Violent No More Workbook

Praise for *Violent No More*

"*Violent No More* is a man-to-man conversation that should be taking place between every father and son, and among men who are true friends with each other. Regardless of whether you are a man looking into his own violence, a woman interested in the problem of domestic abuse, or a professional with years of experience, read this book from start to finish. It offers men who batter the wise voice of guide, thoughtful critic, cheerleader, compassionate coach, and fellow traveler. Michael Paymar courageously invites each man to find his own voice while carefully listening to the voices of women. The stories in this book point us to a hopeful light—men can find the source of real power: respect, equality, trust, love, and nonviolence. Paymar has found the perfect balance between compassion and accountability that we who work with men who batter so fervently seek."

> — John Beams, JD, LSW
> Cofounder of the Center for Nonviolence, Fort Wayne, Indiana

"Finally, someone has written a book for men in offenders groups. *Violent No More* is written to men, using the voices of men. It poses the most central questions to men who batter: How did I get here, and what does it take for me to change?"

> — Ellen Pence, PhD
> Cofounder of the Duluth Domestic Abuse Intervention Project
> and Founder of Praxis International

"This important book speaks frankly to men about domestic abuse. Michael Paymar challenges men to change the beliefs they have about women, power, and relationships. His suggestions give direction and hope. I highly recommend this book to all men who want to stop hurting women."

> — Susan Schecter, MSW
> Author of *Women and Male Violence* and
> *When Love Goes Wrong* (with Ann Jones)

"In this updated edition, Michael Paymar moves our thinking forward by exploring relationships in which men who have battered not only have changed but also have stayed with their partners. His exercises for men who have stopped their violence and are working to transform their relationships are highly recommended. They are also very useful for the general male reader and for counseling programs alike. This is a valuable and courageous work!"

> — Fernando Mederos, EdD
> Director of Fatherhood Engagement,
> Massachusetts Department of Children and Families
> Author of *Programs for Men Who Batter:*
> *Intervention and Prevention* (with Etiony Aldarondo)

"*Violent No More* challenges men who batter to face and change their behavior. This book and workbook are also important for women as they help them better understand their abusive partners. Counselors and domestic violence workers would be wise to make *Violent No More* a must-read for the men in their groups."

— Catherine Waltz, PhD
Barry University School of Social Work

"A highlight of the book is the many inspiring stories by individual men of their violence and their process of change. This book should convince any man that we can and must stop violence against women."

— Paul Kivel, violence-prevention educator
Author of *Men's Work: How to Stop the Violence That Tears Our Lives Apart*

"As a street cop I investigated more domestic abuse cases than I want to remember. I saw the terror in the eyes of the victims. I confronted the offenders who tried to convince me that their behavior was a justified response to provocation. When I became the chief of police in Seattle, I wanted my officers to understand the dynamics of battering. I also wanted to address the fact that, to my dismay, too many of my officers were also perpetrators.

"I read Michael Paymar's groundbreaking book *Violent No More,* which he has thoroughly updated, and have now read his workbook for men who want to change. The book is as important today as when I first read it. Police administrators should read it. Line officers should read it. Men should read it."

— Norm Stamper, former Seattle Chief of Police
Author of *Breaking Rank: A Top Cop's Exposé of the Dark Side of American Policing*

"*Violent No More* presents compelling accounts of men who struggled to end their violence against their partners and describes the changes they made in their thinking and behavior to make that happen. Abusive men will find compassion and hope in these pages, while professionals in the field will find useful strategies to assist men in building loving, nonviolent relationships with their partners and children."

— Denise Gamache
Director, Battered Women's Justice Project

"*Violent No More* joins the small shelf of books that are essential for every therapist and counselor. We therapists *will* encounter abusive men and women who are being abused. We need to understand how to detect the phenomenon of domestic violence and how to intervene, for as Paymar acknowledges, counselors have often been part of the problem rather than the solution. This highly readable, even gripping book is full of stories and exercises (there is now an accompanying workbook), as well as plain, clear speech. Along with books on battered women's experiences, like *When Love Goes Wrong,* this is a must-read for us. Why? Because having this knowledge can save lives!"

— Gus Kaufman Jr., PhD
Licensed Psychologist, Cofounder of Men Stopping Violence, Atlanta, Georgia

"Violent No More fills a void by speaking with authority and authenticity directly to men who batter to challenge their historical and current attitudes, beliefs, and behaviors. It also speaks to women who have lived and are living with men who batter. This book should be on the bench of every judge in the country and on the recommended reading list for probation and parole officers, law enforcement, prosecutors, defense attorneys, magistrates, clergy, social service providers, and members of the health care system."

— David J. H. Garvin, MSW, LMSW
Founder of Alternatives to Domestic Aggression and Batterer
Intervention Services Coalition of Michigan (BISC-MI)

"By hearing directly from both the men and women who've experienced domestic violence and from Michael Paymar, one of the most respected practitioners in the batterer intervention field, readers get a firsthand picture of what domestic violence looks and sounds like in all its forms. They are able to clearly identify the cognitive and behavioral changes required of men who want to change. They also become aware of the safety concerns for survivors.

"As we move into earlier interventions, other professionals—teachers and professors, nurses and doctors, human resources personnel, social workers, psychologists, and faith leaders—will all benefit from this book. It is unfortunate that courses in domestic violence are not part of the core curriculum for graduates in the social work or counseling/psychology fields. *Violent No More* should be required reading for these disciplines."

— Carol Arthur
Executive Director, Domestic Abuse Project, Minneapolis, Minnesota

Author's Note

This workbook is intended to be used in conjunction with the book *Violent No More: Helping Men End Domestic Abuse.*

- ◆ The workbook is for *your* use as you embark upon your new journey. The exercises are to support you in your commitment to stop hurting your intimate partner.

- ◆ The exercises have helped other men just like you who have made the decision to change.

- ◆ The workbook is designed to assist you in evaluating the changes you are making.

- ◆ The workbook is an effective supplement to domestic abuse and counseling programs that work either with court-ordered participants or with men who are attending voluntarily.

Change is difficult, and unfortunately it's too easy to backslide into familiar territory where violence and abusive behavior become normalized—where you use violence to settle conflicts, to stop your intimate partner from doing something, or as punishment. This workbook helps men who have been abusive with an intimate partner reflect on past behaviors, monitor current actions, and take concrete steps to improve their future.

The exercises guide you in exploring your past and present beliefs about violence and abuse, masculinity, women, and what you hope to aspire toward in your present or future intimate relationships. Whether you're currently involved with the person you harmed, are in a new relationship, or are just trying to understand your past actions so you don't repeat them in the future, this workbook will be an important resource for you.

About the Author

Michael Paymar, MPA, has worked in the domestic abuse prevention field for over thirty years. He and his colleague the late Ellen Pence authored the groundbreaking curriculum *Creating a Process for Change for Men Who Batter,* the most widely used treatment model in the world. They worked together at the pioneering Domestic Abuse Intervention Project in Duluth, Minnesota, creating the Duluth Model. He wrote the award-winning documentary *With Impunity: Men and Gender Violence.* As a member of the Minnesota House of Representatives for almost two decades, Michael Paymar authored legislation to combat domestic and sexual abuse and sex-trafficking. In the third edition of *Violent No More* and in this accompanying workbook, Michael provides insight into gender violence and offers hope for men who want to change their behavior and live violence-free lives.

DEDICATION

The *Violent No More Workbook* is dedicated to the work

of the Domestic Abuse Intervention Project in Duluth, Minnesota,

and to the community partners who made this project an international success.

Project Credits

Cover Design: Kelsey Reiman and Brian Dittmar Design, Inc.
Book Production: John McKercher
Copy Editor: Kelley Blewster
Proofreader: Alexandra Mummery
Managing Editor: Alexandra Mummery
Rights Coordinator: Stephanie Beard
Publisher: Todd Bottorff

VIOLENT
no more.

WORKBOOK

Michael Paymar, MPA

Hunter House

An imprint of
Turner Publishing Company

Turner Publishing Company
424 Church Street • Suite 2240 • Nashville, Tennessee 37219
445 Park Avenue • 9th Floor • New York, New York 10022
www.turnerpublishing.com
Copyright © 2015 by Michael Paymar

Manufactured in the United States of America

9 8 7 6 5 4 3 2 1   First Edition   15 16 17 18 19

Contents

Important Note

The material in the *Violent No More Workbook* is intended to provide a guide for men dealing with the issues of domestic abuse. Every effort has been made to provide accurate and dependable information, and the contents of this book have been compiled in consultation with other professionals. However, the reader should be aware that professionals in the field may have differing opinions, and legal policies may differ from state to state and are changing constantly. The publisher, author, and editors cannot be held responsible for any error, omission, professional disagreement, or outdated material.

The ideas, procedures, and suggestions contained in this book are designed to encourage men to work with their personal violence and abusive behavior, but are not intended to replace a professional program. If you have any questions or concerns about applying this information, please consult a domestic abuse intervention program or a licensed therapist. The author and publisher assume no responsibility for any outcome of the use of these materials individually or in consultation with a professional or group.

Acknowledgments

Some of the exercises in this workbook are adapted from the curriculum *Creating a Process of Change for Men Who Batter,* which I created with the late Ellen Pence when we worked together at the Domestic Abuse Intervention Project in Duluth, Minnesota. The Duluth curriculum was revised in 2011 with contributions from Graham Barnes, Barbara Jones-Schroyer, Scott Miller, Carol Thompson, and Lora Wedge. Some exercises were developed when I coordinated the Dakota County Domestic Abuse Program in the Twin Cities metro area and when conducting community training on engaging men in gender-violence prevention.

A special thanks to my wife and partner, Laura Goodman, for her advice, feedback, and support as I developed this workbook. I also would like to acknowledge Kelley Blewster, Alexandra Mummery, Kate Regan, and Laura Goodman for their thoughtful observations in reviewing and editing the book *Violent No More* and this workbook.

Introduction: Before You Begin

I wrote the book *Violent No More: Helping Men End Domestic Abuse* and this, its accompanying workbook, for men who want to stop hurting the ones they love. The book and the workbook offer guidance to men who have been and are violent in relationships with women. They help men understand what is behind their abuse and how to change.

There are many possible reasons why you are using this workbook. You might be concerned that your behavior is hurting the ones you love: your wife or girlfriend, and maybe your children as they observe your violent or abusive behavior. Perhaps you purchased the book and/or the workbook because you know you can't keep doing what you're doing. You know you'll either lose your relationship and your family or end up in serious legal trouble because of your domestic abuse. Your wife or girlfriend may be asking or even telling you to change. She's no longer willing to live with the violence, abuse, and controlling behavior. You now may be ready to do whatever it takes to save the relationship.

Perhaps you've been court ordered to attend a domestic abuse program, or maybe you're attending one voluntarily. *Violent No More* and the *Violent No More Workbook* may be resources recommended by the program or required reading while you're participating. You may have sought help from a counselor or therapist, and he or she may have suggested *Violent No More*. Together the book and workbook are perfect companions for what you're learning in your groups, classes, or counseling sessions.

It won't be easy, but whatever your motivation, take this opportunity to change. Although some of the exercises in this workbook may not seem relevant to your experiences, you should

---

A Note to Women

If your partner is using this workbook and wants you to take part in the exercises, you need to feel comfortable and safe before you agree to do so. If you're still fearful of your partner's behavior, I don't think you should participate. What seems harmless may be dangerous if your partner is still using violence, threats, intimidation, or coercive behavior against you. If your partner is in a domestic abuse program, talk with his counselors to help you decide if the exercises are appropriate for you. If he's not in a program, talk to an advocate or a counselor who is skilled in domestic abuse dynamics to determine if there is any risk in your participating in these exercises. Your partner should honor your decision, whatever it is.

complete them anyway because the material will expose you to new ideas. Your initial reaction might be resistance, and it's okay to feel a little uncomfortable. If you read the book *Violent No More* and complete the exercises in this workbook, I'm confident they will truly guide you toward ending domestic abuse in your life.

I wish you luck on your journey.

How to Use This Workbook

Most of the exercises in the *Violent No More Workbook* are specifically designed to help you understand, monitor, and stop your abusive and controlling behavior. If you put thought and effort into the exercises, you will find them challenging but helpful. Some of the exercises are for men who have stopped battering and want to ensure that they don't backslide or make mistakes with a new intimate partner. Others are designed for couples who are working through basic relationship issues such as negotiating, communicating, compromising, and disagreeing without becoming abusive or controlling.

You will be asked to remember events (some that may be painful) and to write down the thoughts and feelings you had at the time the incident happened. You will be asked to assess the impact your behavior had on your partner, your children (if you have them), your intimate relationship, and, of course, yourself. Some of the exercises require you to only write down a few sentences, and others ask you to do more. My hope is that you will take the time to reflect on the questions and to respond as honestly as possible.

Some of the exercises are a little like journaling (writing in a diary). You may have experience with journaling, but I suspect that most of you don't. Some people religiously write in their journal on a daily basis, documenting events that happened during the day. They record their thoughts, feelings, and goals. I have tried the practice over the years, but I'm not always consistent. When I'm travelling, camping, or in a place of transition, I make it a point to journal regularly. I have kept my journals for years. Reviewing what I wrote a year (or longer) ago can be a powerful experience. I can evaluate the thoughts I had at the time, my hopes for the future, where I'm feeling stuck, and the progress I'm making. I can gain another perspective on the challenges that lie ahead of me.

There are a couple of special places that I visit to get spiritually reconnected—where the world seems to slow down and for the moment everything appears to make sense. Once, I had the luxury of taking two months off from work to focus on writing a book. I visited one of my favorite spots. Every morning I took out my laptop and wrote down my thoughts. Sometimes the process seemed like work and I was quite uninspired. Other times what I was recording seemed to bring me clarity. My words—and taking the time to reflect—allowed me to think through the decisions I had made, both good and bad. I was able to make peace with some of my past mistakes. I realized I couldn't undo them, but I could learn from the experiences. I made written commitments to try new things, even if I knew deep down that accomplishing them might be difficult. Since we're on this earth for such a short time, goals are important, and sometimes we need to take baby steps to reach them. I also use journaling to work on letting go of my anger toward people who I believe have harmed or hurt me.

You don't have to be a good writer to do the exercises in this workbook—or even to keep a journal. More important than what you write is the time you put into thinking about the issues being raised. When you've hurt a person whom you care about, you may feel embarrassed and even ashamed by your behavior; you now want to make things right. By completing the exercises in this workbook and incorporating what you've learned in your domestic abuse group into your life, you will more clearly understand why you hurt or harmed the very person you professed to love. You likely don't want to make those same mistakes again. This workbook will help you become more conscious of what hopefully will be a changing belief system that will help you avoid the kind of destructive thinking and attitudes that led you to be violent in the past.

Ideally you are currently reading the third edition of *Violent No More: Helping Men End Domestic Abuse* and using this workbook in conjunction with the book. The book has many poignant stories of men who, just like you, are going through a journey of change. It offers thorough explanations of the dynamics of domestic abuse that will help you understand where you were, where you are now, and how to get to the place where you are no longer using abusive behavior with your intimate partner. The chapters in the book correspond with the chapters in this workbook. Although most of the material in this workbook is original, I have repeated some relevant material from the main book, mostly quoted passages from men who have participated in domestic abuse groups.

A Note to Counselors

If you are a counselor or a facilitator in a domestic abuse program, ideally you're making the book and workbook available to the men in your groups or the clients you are seeing on an individual basis. Some programs provide the book and workbook to participants as part of their fee; others require participants to purchase the book and workbook, or at least to contribute to the cost.

Some counseling programs use the third edition of *Violent No More* and the *Violent No More Workbook* as supplements to their own curriculum, syllabus, or therapeutic format. The participants carry the book and workbook home with them, read a chapter as homework during the week, and complete the accompanying exercises in the workbook. Some programs use the completed exercises in their group sessions and ask the participants to share what they wrote. It makes for a productive group process.

Some domestic abuse programs use the term "intimate partner violence" or "IPV" rather than "domestic abuse." Many practitioners believe that the term "domestic abuse" can be applied to all kinds of violence in the home, including a parent abusing a child, hence the change in terminology. In this workbook I will continue to use the term "domestic abuse" because it is how most men in our groups define their behavior. I also use the term "men who batter" when I'm talking about men who use violence (even sporadically) and also use other abusive behaviors to control their intimate partners. These behaviors include sexual abuse, intimidation, threats, coercion, isolation, and emotional abuse.

A Challenge for Men

Whenever we're confronted with a difficult personal challenge, finding solutions can seem overwhelming. We know deep down that something needs to change. It helps to recognize that although there are some situations over which we don't have much control, there are many others over which we do. It can be a relief to finally admit that we need to change or get help changing. Sometimes, however, we don't know how to take that first step, and we're afraid to ask for help. This is especially true for men. We can become paralyzed by the challenges facing us, and we can't see even a glimmer of light at the end of the tunnel.

Trust in dreams, for in them is hidden the gate to eternity.
— KHALIL GIBRAN

Domestic abuse creates numerous personal challenges for everyone involved: for the intimate partners who have been abused, for the children who have observed the violence—and also for the men who batter. Thousands of people, primarily women, are killed or seriously injured by their partners every year. Although women sometimes use violence in intimate relationships, the impact of women's violence is usually not the same as men's violence against women. In some jurisdictions there are separate domestic abuse programs for women who have been arrested for assaulting their partners. This workbook is for men, and it addresses men's issues.

If you've been arrested, if you've had a civil order for protection taken out against you, or if your partner has left the relationship, your domestic abuse has been publicly exposed. Chances are many people already knew about your violence. You might feel deeply ashamed by your actions. You may feel betrayed, or you may have convinced yourself that your partner's behavior provoked your actions. You may feel misunderstood and disrespected. *Have you had these thoughts and feelings?*

Like any personal challenge, ending domestic abuse in your life will take a serious commitment and the courage to change. The challenge for you is to:

- recognize that you are solely responsible for your violence

- acknowledge that your violence was intentional and not caused by "losing control," alcohol or drugs, low self-esteem, provocation, or anger

- stop using *all* abusive behaviors (threats, intimidation, coercion, emotional abuse, etc.), which are not only controlling but also can be frightening, especially when you've been violent in the past

- cease minimizing and denying what you've done, and stop blaming your intimate partner for your actions
- understand that your beliefs and attitudes about men, women, and intimate relationships are steeped in sexism and reinforced by our culture
- grasp that your violence has had emotional and psychological impacts on your partner, your children (if you have them), and yourself—and, ideally, gain a sense of empathy about the extent of these impacts
- realize that there are always alternatives to being violent or abusive
- make amends for your past use of violence

Most men in our domestic abuse groups are a bit ambivalent at first. Many think, "I don't really belong in this group. I'm not like these other guys. I'll do what's required, but that's it. I'm not talking about my personal stuff. My wife should be here, not me." Other men keep an open mind. They may be angry or embarrassed, but they're willing to give the program a chance.

Sometimes the men's attitudes change as they continue attending their group. As Andy said:

> An important element in my change process was the way people held me accountable when I got arrested. And that people believed I could change. When I was ordered into the Domestic Abuse Intervention Project, the group leaders and my probation officer all believed in me—that was important to a twenty-one-year-old who was going down the wrong track. When I began the group I was kind of scared. I mean I'd never talked to people about my feelings before, and I'd never been asked the kinds of questions they wanted me to answer. Group process? Bar stools were the closest I ever got to a group. But the process turned out to be comfortable—I wasn't told I was bad, but I did get challenged in a very respectful and helpful way.

My advice is to embark on this process one step at a time. Complete the exercises as best you can. Reflect. Be open to new ideas. Make a commitment to change. Whether you're in a relationship or not, do this for yourself. The rewards will be worth it. Your life is worth it.

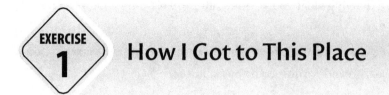

EXERCISE 1

How I Got to This Place

If you are using this workbook, you have most likely committed an act of domestic abuse, or your behavior toward your intimate partner is becoming more abusive. Your partner may be afraid of you. She may be thinking of leaving you. Whether you've been ordered into a domestic abuse group by the courts or you volunteered because you knew you needed help, let's start from the beginning. *Let's explore how you got into this situation in the first place.*

> Before beginning make sure you're in a quiet place where you won't be interrupted. Take some deep breaths to relax and clear your mind.

Part 1: Please review the following example exercise.

Before many of the exercises in this workbook, I have included the responses of men who have been in our domestic abuse groups. The point of these "example" exercises is not to tell you how you should answer the questions but rather to show you how other men have worked through the exercises and ultimately how they have been helped by them.

1. Describe your most recent violent incident or the event that most sticks out in your mind. For many men, this will be the worst episode.

   I had been abusing my wife, Diane, for many years. I slapped her and punched her with a closed fist—lots of violence. I know I've hurt her not only physically but also emotionally by calling her names and putting her down. She put up with the abuse for a long time. A few weeks ago I beat her up pretty bad and was arrested. She had black eyes.

2. What motivated you to seek help? You may have been ordered into a domestic abuse program because you were arrested, or maybe you had a civil order for protection taken out against you. You may have volunteered to participate in a program because you recognized that your behavior was getting more and more destructive.

   The judge ordered me into this program. I have mixed feelings about it, but I really do need to be here. Hopefully I'll learn something. I don't want to lose Diane or go to jail.

Part 2: Please answer the following questions.

1. Describe in detail your most recent violent incident.

_____

_____

_____

_____

_____

_____

_____

2. Explain your motivation to get help.

_____

_____

_____

_____

_____

_____

_____

> If you're in a domestic abuse group, discuss this exercise together, preferably in small groups. Each participant should talk about what he learned from the exercise.

EXERCISE 2   What Do You Hope to Accomplish?

Resistance to taking responsibility for your abusive behavior is a hurdle that you must get over. When some men are ordered into our program, they initially project an attitude of not needing to change. Some men don't want to change. They rigidly hold on to beliefs that their partner's behavior was a justifiable reason for their becoming abusive or violent. They ask, "What would *you* do if your wife/girlfriend did _____?" They desperately try to convince the group counselors and the other participants that they had no other choices given the circumstances. Not only do they blame their partners, but they also accuse the police and the courts of bias for having ordered them into the program.

Some men start new relationships while they're in the program. They initially report how their lives have dramatically improved since they've gotten involved with the new person, justifying to themselves that it was their ex-partner who caused the problems. Because they didn't take the time to reflect on or learn from their past behavior, when relationship issues surface with their new partner, they start abusing again. The cycle begins all over again. Too many men in our groups abuse drugs or alcohol because their lives seem to be unraveling. Some men watch their children act out in inappropriate ways because of what has happened at home, and they don't know what to do.

The longer men stay in the program, the more they start to open up. They observe the progress other men are making and begin taking some personal risks in terms of talking about themselves. They begin to recognize that hurting an intimate partner, regardless of how angry they were at the time, isn't ethically or morally right. Despite their initial bravado and pretending not to care, most men don't really want to end up alone, out of touch with their feelings, and cut off from the company and affection of others—pretty much trapped. *Does this sound familiar? What do you hope to accomplish?*

> Before beginning make sure you're in a quiet place where you won't be interrupted. Take some deep breaths to relax and clear your mind.

Part 1: Please review the following example exercise.

1. Think of some specific changes you believe you need to make in your life in order to become nonviolent and nonabusive in your current or future relationships.

   I'm sort of glad the judge ordered me into these groups. But I'm still mad at Diane. She won't let go of certain things, and we're off to the races. She pushes me. The counselors keep saying that I need to take responsibility for my behavior, so I'll have to work on my attitude.

2. What actions are you willing to take to reach those goals?

I'm going to work hard in these groups. I'm going to be open. I know I need to change. Diane took out a protection order, and now I'm staying at my brother's house. Hopefully we can get the order changed if I make progress.

Part 2: Please answer the following questions.

1. Write down specific changes you believe you need to make in your life in order to become nonviolent and nonabusive in your current or future relationships.

_____

_____

_____

_____

_____

_____

2. What actions are you willing to take to reach those goals?

_____

_____

_____

_____

_____

_____

> **If you're in a domestic abuse group, discuss this exercise together, preferably in small groups. Each participant should talk about what he learned from the exercise.**

A Closing Thought

In this chapter you've explored how you got to this place. Hopefully you've begun to think about what you'd like to accomplish. From time to time, revisit the goals that you outlined in this exercise. As you continue to learn more about yourself, add to this section. Write notes to yourself about your struggles and successes.

I've seldom met a man who has abused his wife or girlfriend who (when he's being brutally honest) can say he's truly happy with his life or the choices he's making. Ultimately each man, whether he's in a domestic abuse group or seeking help on his own, needs to decide if his beliefs and attitudes about women and men are helpful or harmful to having a healthy intimate relationship. Each man needs to find new ways of interacting with an intimate partner in a respectful manner. This takes time and commitment.

Many communities have domestic abuse programs. If you're not in a program, join one. The groups really do work, and you need the support of the counselors and other group members as you start your change process.

The Roots of Men's Violence Against Women

How Our Culture Encourages Violence

Sexism is a practice in which men, and the institutions they control, discriminate against women based on long-held beliefs in male superiority. Although attitudes are changing, sexism still permeates most cultures. We see sexism in the workplace in unequal hiring practices, promotions, and wage gaps. We witness sexism when women are exploited and objectified through sex trafficking (forced prostitution), pornography, and sexual harassment. We observe sexism in the motivation behind domestic and sexual violence. In some countries we see sexism in the examples of forced sterilization, child marriages, war rape, and female genital mutilation. In more subtle ways we experience sexism when men devalue women, dismiss their competence, tell sexual jokes, or use language that demeans them.

> *I am a violent man who learned not to be violent and regrets his violence.*
>
> — JOHN LENNON

The family as an institution has a long history of patriarchy (a family, group, or government controlled by a man or group of men) that has been challenged but not abandoned. As men our beliefs about and stereotypes of masculinity have had a significant influence over how we perceive our role in the family. Whether our role models were our fathers, men who have risen to positions of power, or characters in the media, we learn through observing them and emulating (or rejecting) the behaviors they model. Jason, a participant in our groups, recounted an incident that revealed, at least in part, his father's attitude toward masculinity:

> *I remember my father screaming from the sidelines when I played football in high school. I hated it. It was like winning was so important to him. He was kind of a football star in high school, and he talked about his playing days all the time. Even though he thought he was helping me, you know, giving me encouragement, I just felt like a failure. I'll never forget the time I sprained my ankle in practice. I told him that I'd told the coach I didn't think I could play in the tournament game. He just looked at me with disgust and said, "You goddamned sissy." I'll never forget that.*

In our intimate relationships today, how do disagreements get settled? Who makes the final decision? Who gets the last word? Many men in our groups think the decision should be theirs. They believe there cannot be "two captains of one ship" and that someone has to be in charge.

Some men will say, "If I don't control my wife or girlfriend, she will control me!" These beliefs (or fears) challenge their perceptions of masculinity. Most men recoil when they hear (or imagine being told) belittling statements like, "Who wears the pants in your family?" "What—are you pussy whipped?" or "I'd never let a woman talk to me that way."

Of course, not all men in domestic abuse groups believe in male domination or think that women should be subordinate. Power struggles occur in which both men and women dig in their heels and refuse to budge. Regardless of which camp you fall into, if you've battered your partner, you made the choice to settle disagreements on your terms. You called the shots.

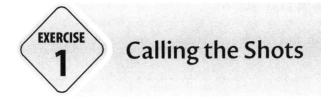

EXERCISE 1

Calling the Shots

This exercise involves recalling an incident in which you felt you needed to "step up to the plate" or "man up" or "take charge" and make a decision about your relationship or the family—even though your decision was contrary to your partner's wishes. *Have there been times when you've called the shots in your intimate relationships? Let's examine what happened.*

> Before beginning make sure you're in a quiet place where you won't be interrupted. Take some deep breaths to relax and clear your mind.

Part 1: Please review the following example exercise.

1. Think about an incident in which you forced a decision on a past partner or on your present partner.

   I cut up our credit cards and closed our checking account. I told her I was going to do it. We just can't continue to get in debt the way we do, so I took some action to change things around our spending. I worked out a budget for food, the kids' expenses, and some basic spending money.

2. How did you justify your behavior?

   Someone had to put a stop to it, and I knew it wouldn't be her. She'll be the first to admit she has no self-control when it comes to money. When we get caught up, maybe we can change.

3. What do you think was the impact on her?

   She was pissed. She'll have to do some things differently until we get caught up. I know she resents me, but I'm not going to end up bankrupted because of her.

4. What do you think was the impact on you?

   I got the problem solved.

5. Looking back, was there a more fair way of resolving the issue? If yes, explain in detail how you might have resolved the issue without imposing your will on your partner.

   Maybe I didn't need to cut up the credit cards, but we needed to do something.

Part 2: Please answer the following questions.

1. Think about an incident in which you forced a decision on a past or present partner.

_____

_____

_____

_____

2. How did you justify your behavior?

_____

_____

_____

3. What do you believe was the impact on her?

_____

_____

_____

4. What do you think was the impact on you?

_____

_____

_____

5. Looking back, was there a more fair way of resolving the issue? If yes, explain in detail how you might have resolved the issue without imposing your will on your partner.

_____

_____

_____

_____

> If you're in a domestic abuse group, discuss this exercise together, preferably in small groups. Each participant should talk about what he learned from the exercise.

A Closing Thought

You may not see yourself as sexist or as someone who believes in male dominance, but many men feel entitled (as though they have expectations or privileges because of their gender) in their relationships with women. Many men believe that they have not only the right but an obligation to make certain decisions in their relationships with intimate partners. They justify these beliefs by claiming they are acting in the best interest of the family. For example, a man in our group told his wife that he didn't want her to socialize with a certain female friend who he believed had a "bad reputation." He defended his right as a husband to demand that she give up this friendship because he thought it reflected poorly on their marriage. Many men (but not all) in the group agreed with his position. After repeated arguments his wife eventually stopped seeing her friend.

Social and cultural norms influence male behavior. In most societies men are expected to be tough, successful, and in control. When men don't meet these stereotypical expectations, they are often judged as weak—by others and themselves. Our jails and prisons are filled with men who have chosen to use violence to resolve disputes with other men and with their intimate partners because they felt disrespected or betrayed.

As men we have important choices to make for ourselves, for our relationships, and about what kind of role models we'll be for our children.

Gender-Based Violence: A Historical Perspective

As men it is important that we understand that men's violence against women isn't a new phenomenon; it has a long history. As I mentioned, attitudes are changing, but our culture still influences our beliefs about what men feel they are entitled to from women. In past generations male domination in the family was expected and even condoned as a way to maintain order. The roles of men and women were well defined: Men were the breadwinners and protectors, and women took care of the household and the family. These functions were reinforced by all community institutions, including places of worship, businesses, community organizations, governments, and the media. In most marriage ceremonies women were expected to agree to "honor" and "obey" their husbands. A woman's obligations included taking care of most domestic duties: cleaning the house, cooking the meals, rearing the children, and responding to the emotional and sexual needs of her husband. Clearly a wife's role was to serve her husband.

You may be thinking that this is ancient history and doesn't apply to men and women today. Although the rules of marriage have changed significantly, and the use of violence to maintain control is no longer outwardly acceptable, in most (but certainly not all) societies, vestiges of the belief that someone in the marriage has to be in charge remain.

Men in our groups struggle over these beliefs. They claim they don't hold these views, but their actions often say otherwise. When they step back and take a wider perspective, they see that their beliefs, like those of most men, are rooted in a long history of male socialization.

Listed below are examples of sexist beliefs, some blatantly so and some more subtle:

- Men are expected to be the head of the household.
- Men should make the major decisions about how money is spent.
- A man can decide what friends his intimate partner has based on his perception of the friends and how they might reflect on the family.
- Men have the right to make decisions about where their partners go and how they dress.
- Men get to decide who does what in the household.
- Men have the right to sex when they want it and how they want it.
- Women really want to be dominated by men.
- Women who challenge male authority are "man haters."

A man's sense of entitlement can come across in ways that are even more subtle. For example, he may:

- decide what the couple talks about or which movies and television shows they watch
- decide when they leave a social event and who drives the car
- believe he has the right to listen to her phone conversations, read her e-mails and texts, and be told what she does during the day
- determine whether she has the right to be angry
- make her financially and emotionally dependent
- decide when an argument is over

A man may enforce these beliefs by:

- threatening to use violence or actually using violence
- making her feel guilty or responsible for their problems
- threatening to leave her
- threatening to take the children if she talks about leaving the relationship
- thinking that violence is justified because that's how men settle problems

In the documentary film that I wrote, *With Impunity: Men and Gender Violence,* my colleague the late Ellen Pence states that violence against women parallels other forms of violence against subordinate groups. She says that group violence is always buttressed by four pillars:

Pillar One: A belief by the dominating group that they are superior to those they dominate, and that God or nature condones their entitlement to a superior role. Every major social structure is designed assuming this to be true, including religion, laws, and cultural expressions in music, movies, literature, fables, and myths.

Pillar Two: The relentless objectification of the dominated group, creating an accepted public discourse that they are dangerous, evil, stupid, lazy, untrustworthy, emotionally and intellectually immature, etc. The message is that keeping the oppressed group down is for the public good.

Pillar Three: Forced submission of the oppressed group to accept their inferior status, requiring enormous effort on the part of the dominating group to control the thinking and emotional reactions of the oppressed group.

Pillar Four: The use of violence with impunity by the dominating group against the oppressed group, and the masking of that violence as something other than an act of domination.

If we look at the ways men have controlled women throughout history, the four pillars are an accurate description of how males have achieved this domination. An individual man may not perceive himself as having this power. In fact, most men in our groups don't see themselves this way at all. Many men have low-paying jobs, dead-end jobs, or no job at all and would question the notion of male dominance. Despite a man's position on the economic ladder, the influence of our sexist society still allows him to feel entitled in relation to women.

Let's examine some of the institutions in our society, including the family, and think about who makes the rules.

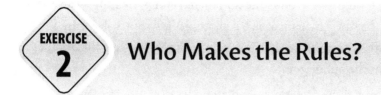

EXERCISE
2

Who Makes the Rules?

Before beginning make sure you're in a quiet place where you won't be interrupted. Take some deep breaths to relax and clear your mind.

We use the pyramid, like the one shown below, to illustrate a hierarchical structure. There are people at the top, in the middle, and at the bottom. Think about examples in history or institutions in our society today where people at the top of the pyramid have power. They typically believe in their own superiority.

Part 1: Please review the following example exercise.

Note: This exercise is designed to be done in a group setting with a counselor facilitating the discussion. If you are completing the exercise alone, the examples will still be helpful in understanding how the family as an institution has historically been structured in such a way that men have more power.

1. Pick an institution, either from history or today, and explain who made/makes the rules. (For example, the criminal justice system, professional sports teams, prisons, colleges/ universities, the military, religious institutions, law enforcement, slavery, a company or business you work/have worked for, etc.)

    Corporations: The CEO/boss/foreman makes the rules.

2. How do people at the top of the pyramid maintain their authority or power?

    They can hire, fire, promote, give raises, and punish employees.

3. How do people at the top justify their position of authority?

    Some people in positions of authority think they're smarter and more qualified.

4. How do people at the bottom of the pyramid feel about their position?

   Most people believe they belong at the bottom.

5. In what ways do people at the bottom blame themselves for being in that position?

   They may feel inferior because they don't have the training or education to be in the middle or at the top of the pyramid.

Part 2: Please answer the following questions.

1. Pick an institution, in history or today, and explain who makes the rules. (For example, the criminal justice system, professional sports teams, prisons, colleges/universities, the military, religious institutions, law enforcement, slavery, a company or business you work/have worked for, etc.)

   _____

   _____

   _____

   _____

   _____

2. How do people at the top of the pyramid maintain their authority or power?

   _____

   _____

   _____

   _____

3. How do people at the top justify their position of authority?

   _____

   _____

   _____

   _____

   _____

4. How do people at the bottom of the pyramid feel about their position?

_____

_____

_____

_____

_____

5. In what ways do people at the bottom blame themselves for being in that position?

_____

_____

_____

_____

In some cases hierarchy is a necessary structure. For instance, in the military or in law enforcement, you need someone to make command decisions and provide discipline in critical incidents. Now think about the *family* as an institution. Until recently the expectation has been that men should be the head of the household; they were at the top of the pyramid. Although things have changed for many families, many men and certainly some women adhere to what we might define as a "traditional family structure" that looks like the hierarchical pyramid above. *Let's examine what the structure was like in your family of origin.*

Part 3: Please answer the following questions.

1. When you were growing up, what did your family structure look like? Who was at the top of the pyramid? Who made the rules? How were the rules enforced?

_____

_____

_____

2. Explain the structure of your current or past relationship. Are/were you at the top of the pyramid? Who makes/made the rules? How are/were they enforced?

_____

3. Can you imagine an intimate family relationship in which the pyramid doesn't exist and both partners are equal? Who would make the rules? Do you see problems with this arrangement?

_____

_____

_____

> If you're in a domestic abuse group, discuss this exercise together, preferably in small groups. Each participant should talk about what he learned from the exercise.

A Closing Thought

Men who have stopped using physical violence in their relationships often describe the difficulty of resolving relationship problems in an amicable way. Later in the workbook we'll discuss ways to negotiate and compromise fairly. But for now, if you are still with the woman you battered, you need to accept that stopping your violence is only the first step to change. Your partner most likely has legitimate fears about whether you've actually changed. She may even be testing you. Assuming you've stopped being violent and you're not using other abusive behaviors, it is important to think about the beliefs you hold about women, relationships, and what being a man means to you. It is a rare man who hasn't been profoundly influenced by our culture, and stepping out of the box can feel risky.

For a long-term relationship to function in a healthy way, inequality must be chipped away at and discarded. In place of power struggles, men and women need to see themselves as partners in the family, as sharing the decision making. This doesn't mean that a man and a woman can't construct their own roles in their relationship or marriage. As I stated in the book *Violent No More,* for example, I know couples who take turns working so that one person can spend more time with the children, go back to school, or become involved in community or social-change activities. They make financial agreements and don't place a higher value on the person who is providing most of the income. For many couples, economic realities make this difficult, but some do manage, and they don't have a conflict with the arrangement; in fact, it frees them up to do other things they believe are valuable.

Having a real partnership in an intimate relationship may seem foreign to you, but if you're committed to change, the benefits will be well worth it.

How We Learn to Be Violent

The Violence We Learn at Home

Many researchers in the domestic abuse field conclude that men learn to use violence by what they observed or experienced as children. They see their fathers use violence with no negative repercussions for their actions, and they receive the message that this kind of behavior gets results and is an acceptable response to conflict. When Adrian Peterson, a star football player with the Minnesota Vikings, was charged with child abuse for using a tree branch to give his four-year-old son a "whopping," the country became embroiled in a discussion about what constitutes appropriate discipline. Most professionals will state clearly that physical punishment of a child not only is ineffective but also teaches children that violence is acceptable.

> *Victory attained by violence is tantamount to defeat.*
>
> — MAHATMA GANDHI

As stated in the book *Violent No More,* when a child witnesses his mother being physically abused, the message the child gets is that the father is in charge. He seems all-powerful. Sometimes the child may sense there is something wrong with the father's behavior; at other times he may conclude that his father has a rational reason for becoming so angry and abusive. One man in our group stated that he couldn't understand why his mother wouldn't just shut up when his parents were arguing, because he knew she'd get hit if she persisted. Some men thought that the violence they grew up with seemed normal because it was all they experienced. Others talked about the trauma of witnessing someone they loved being harmed.

Hector, a man I interviewed in *Violent No More,* said:

> *One time I helped my father make this leather belt. I thought we were making it together for Scouts and this was part of the project. But then he hung it up on the wall and said, "This is the belt I'll be beating you with." And he did. He would hit me with the belt, and if I cried, he'd scream, "Stop crying, you're a man! You're not a girl, stop crying!" Eventually the belt broke and I wasn't crying anymore. He said, "Okay, now that you're not crying and you don't need the belt, I'm going to treat you like a man." At first I didn't know what that meant. I thought maybe there would be some relief. But it turned out what he really meant was that from now on he would hit me with his fists, because men hit with their fists. So I learned not to put my head down, because if I did, that was a sign of inferiority and weakness.*

Men in our groups have said they vowed not to repeat the domestic abuse they saw as children. However, for many of them, when conflicts arose with their partners and they felt they could not win or control the situation with words, they mimicked the abusive behavior of their fathers. With a hit or a punch they could end an argument just like their fathers did. And if there are no consequences for the violence—such as getting arrested or losing the relationship—the behavior becomes reinforced. Of course, not all boys who witnessed domestic abuse at home use violence against their intimate partners as adults, but the risk does increase. *Does any of this seem familiar? How did you learn about violence?*

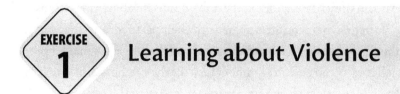

Learning about Violence

Before beginning make sure you're in a quiet place where you won't be interrupted. Take some deep breaths to relax and clear your mind.

Part 1: Please answer the following questions.

Think back to the first time you witnessed someone being physically hurt by another person. This incident doesn't necessarily have to be one that took place in your childhood, but it may be. Some examples might include one parent assaulting another parent, a parent hitting your sibling, a fight between your siblings, a bully being violent to a friend or schoolmate, the police arresting someone who is resisting, etc.

1. Try to recall the incident in detail. What was your reaction to the violence?

_____

_____

_____

_____

_____

_____

_____

2. How did you feel while you witnessed it? How did you feel afterward?

_____

_____

_____

_____

_____

_____

_____

3. Did you talk to anyone about what you saw or how you felt (e.g., a family member, teacher, friend, police officer, etc.)?

_____

_____

_____

_____

_____

_____

In one of our groups, a counselor had the following discussion with a group member named Reggie about the impact of witnessing violence. The counselor asked Reggie how he felt when he saw his father beating his brother for stealing a car:

> **Reggie:** I was horrified. I'd never seen anyone get punched like that close up except on TV. I remember my brother covering up his head to shield himself from the blows. I felt totally powerless to do anything. I realized he probably deserved to be punished for stealing the car, but even at my young age I could tell the beating was severe.
>
> **Counselor:** Were you surprised by the fury of your father's anger?
>
> **Reggie:** I was definitely surprised by his anger and his actions. I'm not sure what the lasting impact was on me, except maybe the experience made me conscious about never getting so angry at my children that I could resort to violence like my father did that night.

Part 2: Please answer the following questions.

Think of a time when you were the victim of violence as a child or adult. If you have never been a victim of violence, describe a situation in which someone was very abusive toward you in a manner that made you feel scared or intimidated.

1. What was your reaction to the situation?

_____

_____

_____

_____

_____

_____

2. How did you feel during the incident? How did you feel after the incident?

_____

_____

_____

_____

_____

3. Did you talk to anyone about what happened?

_____

_____

_____

_____

_____

In one of our groups, a counselor had the following discussion with participant Roland about being a victim of violence:

> **Counselor:** *You said you felt powerless during the mugging. Do you really think you had any other option?*
> **Roland:** *I think most men fantasize that they could do something heroic. My fantasy is that I had a black belt in karate. I can visualize my hits and kicks as I take these two guys down. Just like in the movies.*
> **Counselor:** *So because you couldn't be like Clint Eastwood you saw yourself as a failure?*
> **Roland:** *In part because my wife was there, I felt like less of a man.*
> **Counselor:** *How did your wife react to you after the incident?*
> **Roland:** *Well, both she and the police kept emphasizing that we had no other options, but I still wished I'd done something. It's amazing how men are socialized about violence. I think most of us are horrified when we're confronted with it, but we feel that somehow we should be able to stand up to any challenge.*
> **Counselor:** *Does that experience affect you today?*
> **Roland:** *Sure. I think about it and my inaction a lot. I'm nervous walking in certain parts of town. If I see more than one man coming toward me, I start to prepare. I'm much more sensitive to the psychological impact of violent crime on victims.*

> If you're in a domestic abuse group, discuss this exercise together, preferably in small groups. Each participant should talk about what he learned from the exercise.

EXERCISE 2

The Violence We Learn from Society

As boys we learn a great deal about the use of violence from the culture in which we live. When I was growing up, we played imaginary games of war with plastic rifles, competed in violent sports, read violent comic books, and couldn't get enough of violent movies. Today boys play violent video games and are exposed to violent pornography with the click of a mouse on their computers. We are taught at an early age that violence is an acceptable way to handle conflict. If we refrained from using violence, we might have been ridiculed by other boys. If this occurs, most boys feel they aren't measuring up.

It is difficult to determine how these childhood experiences and cultural messages impact us as we mature into men. Just like witnessing domestic abuse at home as a child, it's hard to imagine that the violence we learn from society doesn't shape who we are, especially for men who are constantly exposed to violence in their communities.

Violence is powerful, especially if it subdues those whom it's used against.

Mark, a man in one of our groups, told me that he didn't witness domestic abuse in the home, as so many other men had. He told me that he slapped his girlfriend because he wanted to fit in with his friends in high school; they were slapping their girlfriends. One day when he saw his girlfriend talking to another boy, he slapped her, and she started crying. He said that on the one hand he felt bad, but on the other hand he felt good; punishing his girlfriend gave him a sense of power.

In the same way that some males learn violence in the home, Mark (and many other men) learned violence from society. Let's dig a bit deeper into this topic. *What messages about violence have you gotten from society? Have they had an impact on you or your intimate relationships?*

> Before beginning make sure you're in a quiet place where you won't be interrupted.
> Take some deep breaths to relax and clear your mind.

Part 1: Please review the following examples of violence in mass media.

- professional wrestling in which women are sexualized or humiliated
- video games in which women are beaten, raped, or killed
- music with lyrics that describe hurting, raping, or punishing women
- pornography in which women are forced to do sexually demeaning things or are physically or sexually abused

Part 2: Please answer the following questions.

1. List several forms of mass media that you have watched or listened to that are violent or have violent messages about women (e.g., music, movies, television, social media, video games, sports, etc.).

_____

_____

_____

_____

2. Have the messages or images had an impact on you? If yes, in what ways?

_____

_____

_____

_____

3. Do you think these kinds of images have an impact on boys and young men? If yes, how?

_____

_____

_____

_____

4. What impact do you think these images and messages have on girls and women?

_____

_____

_____

_____

> If you're in a domestic abuse group, discuss this exercise together, preferably in small groups. Each participant should talk about what he learned from the exercise.

Why We Use Violence

As I pointed out in the book *Violent No More,* violence produces immediate results. It works, in a perverse sort of way. Except in cases of real self-defense, I have never met a man who battered who would dispute the fact that his motive in being violent was to: (1) stop his partner from saying or doing something he disapproved of, (2) shut her up, or (3) punish her for doing something he didn't like.

Participating in a domestic abuse group can help some men understand how growing up male in this culture has influenced their beliefs about women and relationships. Others, especially those who grew up in violent households, may need to see a counselor or a therapist to unravel some of the past and finally say good-bye to it. Regardless of how you got where you are, you alone are responsible for what you do next. It is helpful—sometimes even necessary—to understand your past, but it is completely up to you to take charge of your present and future.

The following is a variation of an exercise I designed with my colleague the late Ellen Pence when we worked together at the Domestic Abuse Intervention Project.

> Before beginning make sure you're in a quiet place where you won't be interrupted. Take some deep breaths to relax and clear your mind.

Please answer the following questions.

1. Think about a time when you used violence against your past or present partner. Choose an incident that really stands out in your mind—maybe the incident you're most ashamed of—and describe what happened and what you did. If you have not been violent, think of a time when your behavior was very intimidating: You screamed in her face, pounded your fist on a table, hit a wall, or threw something at or close to your partner. Describe the incident in detail.

_____

_____

_____

_____

_____

2. Explain the purpose of your violence in the incident you just described. In other words, what did you want to have happen?

_____

_____

_____

_____

_____

3. What were the short-term and long-term impacts of the violence on your partner, yourself, and the relationship?
Short-term impacts:

_____

_____

_____

Long-term impacts:

_____

_____

_____

Reread your answer to question 2. Your purpose for being abusive was probably to gain something very specific, like stopping an argument or getting your way.

Now look at question 3, on the short- and long-term impacts of your violent or threatening behavior. You will probably notice two things. In the short term you most likely got what you wanted, at least initially. Your partner may have stopped arguing, not gone out, or otherwise altered her behavior. However, in the longer term you likely got the exact opposite of what you wanted. Your partner may have become distant, or intimacy may have diminished. She probably became furious with you for your behavior and may have contemplated leaving the relationship.

Does this coincide with your experience? If yes, explain.

_____

_____

_____

_____

In one of our groups, the counselor discussed the use of violence with a man named T.J.:

> **T.J.:** *I remember slapping my daughter Elisha hard. I couldn't believe I did it. She was in shock, and the look she gave me was one of total disbelief, almost betrayal. She ran from the room screaming.*
> **Counselor:** *How did she respond to you afterward?*
> **T.J.:** *She was actually concerned about how upset I was. I apologized and promised her I would never allow my anger to get to that point again.*
> **Counselor:** *Do you think that slap changed things?*
> **T.J.:** *Well, I think some of the innocence of our father–daughter relationship changed. I also became very aware of my temper and my ability to be violent. We've had many arguments since, but I'm very conscious of what I'm capable of because of that incident.*

> **If you're in a domestic abuse group, discuss this exercise together, preferably in small groups. Each participant should talk about what he learned from the exercise.**

A Closing Thought

In this chapter's exercises so far, we have explored how the violence we learned at home or from the culture can have a profound impact on us as adults. If you had a hurtful or neglectful childhood, it is important that you not blame your past for your actions today. For one thing, holding on to painful childhood experiences might make you distrustful of intimacy; you may get easily defensive because you're in survival mode. If this seems familiar to you, get help from a counselor. You can work through these feelings and painful memories. Regardless of how and where you learned about violence, you must address your current way of reacting to women in relationships, because that is something you *can* change. We make a personal choice to become violent regardless of what we've been exposed to in our childhoods.

There is disagreement among researchers about the long-term impact of watching violence on television or in movies, playing violent video games, and looking at violent pornography, all of which are so easily accessible. But it's hard to imagine that boys and young men aren't desensitized by the constant exposure to gratuitous violence and the degradation of women. It's also hard to imagine that the objectification of women through demeaning music and pornography doesn't have an impact on intimacy.

We make choices despite what we've been exposed to in our homes and by society. *Today we can choose to reject violence and stop hurting the ones we love.*

Sexual Violence

In domestic abuse groups, men are often hesitant to discuss sexual abuse. They may have trouble identifying certain behaviors as sexually abusive, or they experience discomfort talking about the issue in a group setting. For instance, a man in our groups may describe an incident in which he pressured his partner to have sex. He might not see that behavior as abusive or make any connection to his past use of violence and her submission to sex. He may defend his behavior by saying that he didn't force her. Some men in our groups will admit to pressuring their partners to perform sexual acts that they viewed on pornography. They defend their position by saying that their partners weren't put off by pornography. Some men will equate sex after a violent incident as confirmation that the violence wasn't that bad, that his partner really loves him despite the abuse, or that the sex was proof she had forgiven him. His sense of reality doesn't seem to match up to what battered women are saying.

Sylvie, whom I interviewed for the book *Violent No More,* talked about her experiences with the man who abused her. As she said:

> To me it's the ultimate in control when a man has sex with you after he's beaten you. I think Tyler had this strange way of equating sex with negative attitudes about women—basically a woman's function was for the sexual pleasure of men. It was all very confusing for me. Here this man beats me, and then he's making love to me.
>
> Tyler raped me many times, although I'm not sure he saw it that way. Sometimes when he had friends over he would make derogatory sexual comments about me. I felt humiliated and violated.

Cassie, another woman whose story appears in *Violent No More,* also talked about the sexual abuse that occurred during her marriage:

> I learned very early that I had no choice. Sometimes he would force himself on me. I told him I wasn't going to respond sexually, but he didn't seem to care. That really reinforced this whole thing that he didn't care how he was getting sex. It didn't matter to him if I participated or not. It was the ultimate in objectification.
>
> I either had sex or I got beaten up. I never saw it as sexual abuse at the time. Whenever we had a fight it was never completely over until we had sex. Even when I was feeling rotten I had to submit, and for him everything was supposedly okay.

We all get mixed messages about sexuality when we're growing up. As boys we learn about sex from other boys, from siblings, from movies, and, for many, by viewing pornography. The discussion that some boys have with their parents about sex (I never did) is about as helpful as the health class explanations I was forced to listen to in junior high school. (There was usually an uncomfortable male teacher with slides and films explaining sexual acts in very academic terms. We—boys and girls were separated—all chuckled in amusement or embarrassment).

For boys (and for girls in different ways) our hormones and sexual urges were exploding, and there was intense pressure to have sexual experiences (conquests) with girls. We constantly talked about sex. In my circle there were "good girls" and "bad girls," but as boys we were always expected to be chasing. We joked, ridiculed other boys who hadn't "scored," and lied about our own "accomplishments." When we had serious girlfriends, we were relentless and used various forms of pressure to have sex. Most of us didn't know what being "sexually respectful" meant, because it was never explained, so we figured out a way to get our "needs" met. The temporary satisfaction was often followed by disappointment and, for some, guilt.

As boys become young men, the pressure to have sex intensifies, as does male bonding around sexual conquests. The news of rape on college campuses and in the military has resulted in serious discussions about the behavior of some men who have a sense of entitlement when it comes to sex. The use of date-rape drugs, plying women with alcohol, and sexual assault have called into question the ethical responsibilities of men, of our institutions of higher learning, and of the armed forces. Many women don't report being sexually assaulted because of the stigma and because they don't think they'll be believed. This is not to say that young women on college campuses and in the military are not partying and engaging in sexual activity. They are. But when men cross the line and the sex becomes nonconsensual, the behavior is a sexual assault.

A woman named Joyce told me in an interview about being raped in the military:

> I didn't report it, because I knew nobody was going to believe me. Secondly, as in most rapes, I knew this person well. I let him into my home. I had a tremendous amount of guilt over what happened, and I also ended up pregnant. I knew if I reported the rape, I would lose the opportunity to become an officer and it would jeopardize my career. So I stayed silent.
>
> You're isolated. You want to be part of the group. And now you've been sexually assaulted, and who are you going to tell? Even if you have the courage to report, the people you are telling are directly responsible for not just your career but also your housing, your pay, your food—your whole lifeline. It's very much like incest.

Men go to strip clubs, pay women for sex, view pornography—and see all of this as normal male behavior. We are socialized to believe that "boys will be boys" and this is what men do. We can't just dismiss this conduct as harmless behavior.

I don't want to leave the impression that I think all men are dragging their knuckles on the ground as if we haven't evolved from the Stone Age. In intimate, loving relationships, men and women are sexually respectful and want mutually shared sexual pleasure. Partners communicate about sex, are affectionate, compliment each other, recognize each other's sexual needs, and express love and intimacy in many ways. Of course, even in healthy relationships there are challenges. Pregnancy, children, stress, physical problems, and a lack of time can impact intimacy. Couples can get bored and lazy, which impacts the commitment they put into making sure there's sexual fulfillment. In a sexually respectful relationship, problems are discussed and solutions can be found.

When a man batters an intimate partner, everything changes. Intimacy and respectful sexuality often (but not always) devolve into sexual abuse. Sex becomes another tactic. Men who batter might become sexually abusive, force inappropriate behavior, use sex to humiliate and degrade, and, as mentioned earlier, use it to absolve themselves of guilt or responsibility for their violence. In interviews with battered women at the Domestic Abuse Intervention Project in Duluth, 50 percent of the women whose partners were in our program claimed that they had experienced sexual abuse in their relationship. As Jim, a man in our groups, said, "When I wanted sex, we had it, and there was no flak about it."

This topic may be difficult to discuss, but it's important that we do. Whether you stay with your current partner or get involved with someone new in the future, being sexually respectful is an essential goal.

Does some of this discussion resonate with you? Let's examine what it means to be sexually respectful in an intimate relationship.

Being Sexually Respectful

The following exercise is for men who *choose* and *want* a respectful sexual relationship. The goal is to avoid using coercive or abusive behaviors in your sexual relationship.

At the end of the exercise (and in the exercises in the following chapter) you will be asked to commit to changing your behavior in what's called a Life-Changing Plan. It is a way to *practice* what you are committing to change. Later you will be asked to return to your plan and *assess* your progress. The plan is simple. It's an honest commitment to change something in your life—a behavior, an attitude, negative thoughts—to help you stay on course in your commitment to change. If you are in a domestic abuse group, your counselors may modify these exercises and/or the process used for assessing change.

In this exercise you will be asked to think about a time when you were sexually abusive or sexually disrespectful. You'll examine your reasons for using these behaviors. In other words, why did you do what you did? You'll be asked to think about the short- and long-term impacts of your actions on your partner and yourself, and to compare those negative or abusive experiences with times when you were sexually respectful and considerate. Finally, you will state what you're willing to commit to in your Life-Changing Plan in order to be sexually respectful in the future. *Even though this topic is sensitive, I encourage you to work through the exercise.*

> Before beginning make sure you're in a quiet place where you won't be interrupted. Take some deep breaths to relax and clear your mind.

Part 1: Please review the following examples of sexually abusive behavior.

Examples of sexually abusive or inappropriate behavior

- expected sex even though she didn't want it
- pressured her to do things she didn't feel comfortable with
- made her watch pornography
- inserted objects into her vagina or anus against her will
- used violence during sex
- forced her to have sex while she was sleeping
- threatened to send pictures or videos of her nude or having sex to others in order to gain her compliance

Examples of demeaning sexual behavior

- compared her body to other women's

- made her feel bad about her body and her sexual abilities
- made degrading sexual statements
- made her pose for pictures or took videos of her when she didn't feel comfortable
- accused her of having affairs when she did something different sexually
- called her sexually demeaning names

Examples of controlling sexual behavior

- told her you'd "get it" elsewhere if she didn't submit
- used sex as a reward
- blamed her when you weren't satisfied
- didn't care if she was satisfied
- disclosed intimate information about her in public
- wanted sex after you'd been violent, and expected her to forgive you

Part 2: Please answer the following questions.

1. List several incidents when you were sexually abusive, inappropriate, demeaning, or controlling. (If you're uncomfortable writing these incidents in your workbook, write them on a separate piece of paper that you can discard if you want.)

_____

_____

_____

2. Pick an incident from your list that most stands out in your mind. Describe it.

_____

_____

_____

_____

3. What was the purpose of your behavior? Describe what you were feeling and thinking.

_____

_____

_____

4. What were the short-term and long-term impacts of your behavior?
   Short-term impacts:

   _____

   _____

   _____

   Long-term impacts:

   _____

   _____

   _____

5. Looking back at the incident, what could you have done differently to avoid being sexually abusive, inappropriate, demeaning, or controlling?

   _____

   _____

   _____

   _____

   _____

Part 3: Please review the following examples of practicing and assessing one's progress.

1. **Practicing: Making a life-changing plan for being sexually respectful.** Think of ways you can be sexually respectful with your current or future intimate partner. How can you talk about sex, intimacy, your needs, and her needs?

   I'll apologize for my past behavior and commit to being sexually respectful in the future. If my partner is open to having the discussion, I hope we can talk about what it means to be sexually respectful and intimate. I won't pressure her in any way. I won't make sexual jokes that I know make her uncomfortable.

2. **Assessing your progress.** Return to this section of your workbook after several weeks of following your plan, and write down the results of your changed behavior.

   We have been talking more about sexual respect. I haven't expected sex or pressured her into sex after we've been arguing. Since I've been attending the groups I'm more aware that men and women have different needs, perceptions, and expectations.

Part 4: Please answer the following questions.

1. **Practicing:** Think of ways you can be sexually respectful with your current or future intimate partner. How can you talk about sex, intimacy, your needs, and her needs?

_____

_____

_____

_____

_____

2. **Assessing your progress:** Return to this section of your workbook after several weeks of following your plan, and write down the results of your changed behavior.

_____

_____

_____

_____

_____

> If you're in a domestic abuse group, discuss this exercise together, preferably in small groups. Each participant should talk about what he learned from the exercise.

A Closing Thought

As I stated in _Violent No More,_ as men, when we examine our sexual behavior, most of us have done things that we now wish we hadn't, whether in our youth or as adults. We may have taken advantage of women or used them for sex. We may have gone to a strip show, paid for sex, or viewed pornography. We may have pressured a partner to have sex. Maybe you still think that some of those activities are okay.

For me, stepping back and looking at my own past behaviors with the knowledge I have today, I more fully understand how much influence the culture had on me and on other men. I now understand that because I _can_ do certain things doesn't make them right. As men, most of us have bought into stereotypes. We have believed that prostitution is a victimless crime or that stripping and pornography are free-will choices made by women. The majority of women being trafficked (prostituted) have not chosen that profession. They are being exploited, and many are being coerced. As men, let's have the courage to reject this behavior.

It's More than Physical Violence

The Tactics of Men Who Batter

Domestic abuse, and more specifically battering, is more than physical and sexual violence. At the Domestic Abuse Intervention Project, battered women in support groups made a list of the abusive behaviors used by the intimate partners who battered them: how they were silenced, scared, manipulated, confused, and controlled. These actions are represented by the Power and Control Wheel, on the opposite page. You will note that physical and sexual violence are on the rim of the wheel. They hold the wheel together. The behaviors inside the wheel are the tactics that many men who batter use to get their way. Power and control are in the center of the wheel, because that is the reason for being abusive or violent.

> *Anger is that powerful force that blows out the light of reason.*
>
> — RALPH WALDO EMERSON

The word "battering" refers to the systematic use of abusive behaviors, including physical violence, to establish and maintain control over another person. Ending your use of physical violence is the first step in your process of change, but you must also commit to ending other types of abusive behavior.

To see how this applies to you, take a look at each section of the Power and Control Wheel and examine the examples listed. Can you think of times when you've used a number of these behaviors? Most people can identify with some of the behaviors on the wheel. But there is an important distinction between what happens in relationships in which physical violence has never occurred and in those in which it has. When physical violence has been used in the past, all of the other behaviors on the Power and Control Wheel change. Anger, words, and actions take on a new meaning. I remember a woman telling me that her husband punched her in the face when they were first married and at the same time screamed at her with incredible intensity. Her husband never hit her again in their twenty-year marriage, but when he was upset with her, he would use the same voice he'd used the night he'd hit her, causing her to freeze. The memory of the blow he'd struck haunted her for years, but he never hit her again; he didn't need to.

Andy, a participant in our groups, describes a method he used to intimidate his partner:

> *If we were at a party and my partner was talking to another man, I would just look at her, and she would be at my side. No one knew what was going on. It was just a look or a crooked smile and she knew.*

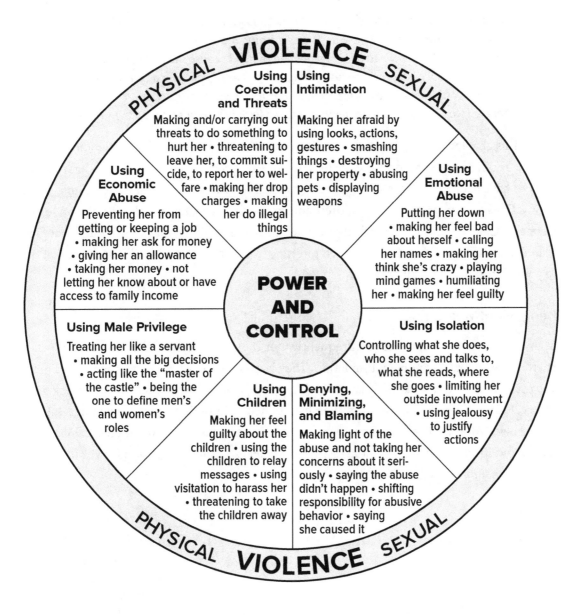

The figure shows a circular diagram. Around the outer ring reads: **PHYSICAL VIOLENCE SEXUAL** (top) and **PHYSICAL VIOLENCE SEXUAL** (bottom). The center circle reads **POWER AND CONTROL**. The wheel contains eight segments:

Using Coercion and Threats
Making and/or carrying out threats to do something to hurt her • threatening to leave her, to commit suicide, to report her to welfare • making her drop charges • making her do illegal things

Using Intimidation
Making her afraid by using looks, actions, gestures • smashing things • destroying her property • abusing pets • displaying weapons

Using Emotional Abuse
Putting her down • making her feel bad about herself • calling her names • making her think she's crazy • playing mind games • humiliating her • making her feel guilty

Using Economic Abuse
Preventing her from getting or keeping a job • making her ask for money • giving her an allowance • taking her money • not letting her know about or have access to family income

Using Male Privilege
Treating her like a servant • making all the big decisions • acting like the "master of the castle" • being the one to define men's and women's roles

Using Isolation
Controlling what she does, who she sees and talks to, what she reads, where she goes • limiting her outside involvement • using jealousy to justify actions

Using Children
Making her feel guilty about the children • using the children to relay messages • using visitation to harass her • threatening to take the children away

Denying, Minimizing, and Blaming
Making light of the abuse and not taking her concerns about it seriously • saying the abuse didn't happen • shifting responsibility for abusive behavior • saying she caused it

Sylvie, who was quoted earlier, explains how intimidation creates immediate fear:

When Tyler was angry at me, he would walk around me while he was talking or yelling so I never knew what to expect. I'd try to maintain eye contact with him because he had hit me in the back of the head before. He wouldn't necessarily have to be talking angrily, but the fact that I had to turn around and watch him was very intimidating. He knew exactly what he was doing.

If you have used physical violence in the past, the behaviors on the wheel (some might even call them tactics) are the wild card that can be played at any time. Even if you have no intention of using physical violence, your partner doesn't know that. Many men fail to recognize the impact of the abusive acts identified on the Power and Control Wheel; a man is still battering unless he stops using *all* of these behaviors. As group participant Jim said:

I married Gretchen...after a very short courtship.... My violence toward her was mostly grabbing her by the arms and pushing her down. I think I only hit her once. I really didn't have to be very violent with her, because she was submissive, and I could make her afraid by just yelling at her. I would give her a certain look, and she would know I was upset. In that marriage I was the ultimate ruler. I don't believe I was ever in love with her, but I stayed with her because it was convenient.

In this chapter we're going to examine many of the behaviors on the Power and Control Wheel. You'll be asked to look at your reasons for using them. In other words, what did you want to have happen? You'll also be asked to think about the short- and long-term impacts of your actions on your partner, your children, and yourself. And finally, as in the exercise on sexual respect in Chapter 3, you will be asked to commit to changing your behavior in a Life-Changing Plan. It is a way to *practice* what you are committing to change. Later you will be asked to return to your plan and *assess* your progress.

Being Nonthreatening

Many men use physical violence infrequently, but they abuse women by resorting to other coercive behaviors, including intimidation. They learn how to intimidate women, other men, and their children. Some use body language. They glare, tower over their partners, or block their physical space. Some men slam down their fists, punch walls or doors, or throw things. Intimidating behavior is frightening; the person being intimidated is never sure if physical violence will follow. *Remember a time when you used intimidation to control your partner. Let's examine how you can be nonthreatening in the future.*

Being Nonthreatening

The following exercise is for men who *choose* and *want* to be nonthreatening with their current or future intimate partners and with their children. The goal is to stop using intimidating and threatening behavior to get what you want.

> Before beginning make sure you're in a quiet place where you won't be interrupted. Take some deep breaths to relax and clear your mind.

Part 1: Please review the following examples of intimidation and the sample exercise below.

Examples of physical intimidation

- punched walls and doors
- slammed tables
- threw things
- destroyed property
- displayed weapons
- crowded her space

Examples of intimidating body language

- glared, stared, gave her angry looks
- pointed
- made a fist

Examples of intimidating language

- raised my voice, screamed
- gave her the silent treatment
- left a threatening note
- talked in a way I knew would scare her

The following sample exercise is from Bill, a group participant.

1. List several incidents when you used intimidation with a past or current partner.

   Threw things, pounded on the table, screamed at my wife and kids.

2. Pick the incident from your list that stands out most in your mind. Describe the incident in detail.

> *Sometimes I get really angry if the house is in disarray, especially on the weekends when I'm home and I want to relax a little. I don't believe I should have to remind the kids to do things, and if I say anything to my wife, Kathy, we end up arguing. One time the house was a mess—dirty dishes in the sink and stuff lying around— so I started pounding my fist on the kitchen table and went from room to room screaming at the kids. When Kathy tried to intervene, I came at her like I was going to hit her. I just stood there screaming and swearing at her for not getting on the kids.*

3. What was the purpose of your behavior? Describe what you were feeling and thinking.

> *I wanted the house to be clean and orderly. I thought the kids were being disrespectful by not keeping the place clean. I also thought Kathy was enabling the kids' behavior by not doing more to enforce the rules. I felt disrespected and angry.*

4. What were the short-term and long-term impacts of your behavior?
   Short-term impacts:

> *When I pounded on the table and started screaming, everyone was scared. The kids started picking things up and doing what I was demanding. Kathy tried to calm me down, but when I screamed at her I'm sure she was afraid, because I've hit her for stupid things when I was upset.*

   Long-term impacts:

> *We had planned on having a family dinner that night, but the whole day was ruined because of my outburst. Kathy wouldn't talk to me, and the kids avoided me the rest of the day and that evening. On the weekends I've noticed that the kids will try to make plans so they don't have to be at home, because of me.*

5. Looking back at the incident, what could you have done differently to avoid being intimidating, even if you were upset? If you are in a group, ask the group members or the counselors for ideas.

> *I could have waited for a time when I wasn't upset, talked with Kathy about how I was feeling, and then worked out a plan with her. After we agreed on a plan, we could both have talked to the kids. I could have taken a time-out when I was feeling agitated.*

6. **Practicing: Making a life-changing plan for being nonthreatening.** Briefly explain what you will commit to doing in order keep yourself from being intimidating with your partner or your children in the future.

> *Kathy and I did agree on some basic rules about keeping the house clean and how we would ensure that the kids did their fair share. We had a family meeting, and the kids reluctantly went along with the plan. I've also tried to be aware of my*

agitation level, because even though the family agreed to things, I still think the kids should do more. I have been talking about my intimidating behavior in my group to get help.

7. **Assessing your progress.** Return to this section of the workbook after several weeks of following your plan, and write down the results of your changed behavior.

> *I've taken time-outs and gone down to the neighborhood Y [to work out] when I've gotten agitated. I haven't gotten upset with Kathy or the kids for several weeks, but they still seem nervous around me, especially on the weekends.*

Note: The Time-Out Rules are listed on page 103.

Bill asked for help from the group. The group members thought he should have talked over his feelings and expectations about the house with Kathy when he wasn't upset. They thought that Bill and Kathy could have come up with an acceptable and workable plan, held a family meeting, and outlined some basic ground rules for the house.

The group also discussed that it was possible that Bill was overreacting and that his expectations might be too high. Bill wasn't certain about this, but he said he was willing to think about it. Several group members gave similar examples of letting things build up and then "going off" on someone. The group thought Bill should have taken a time-out when he started getting agitated.

When Bill asked the group for suggestions, he was quite sincere in wanting to change an aspect of his life he found troubling. I remember him saying to the group that he truly didn't want his family to be afraid of him anymore. He also thought Kathy *shouldn't* be fearful anymore because he was attending his groups.

Change takes time. Each family member's perception of whether you have actually changed will vary. You must give people time to observe your behavior; it's only when your family begins to feel safe that trust can be restored. The fact that Bill stopped pounding on the table and screaming about the house being in disarray will not erase his family's memories of those intimidating times. He needs to be patient.

Part 2: Please answer the following questions.

1. List several incidents when you have used intimidation with a past or current partner.

_____

_____

_____

_____

_____

2. Pick the incident from your list that most stands out in your mind. Describe it in detail.

_____

_____

_____

_____

_____

3. What was the purpose of your behavior? Describe what you were feeling and thinking.

_____

_____

_____

_____

4. What were the short-term and long-term impacts of your behavior?
   Short-term impacts:

_____

_____

_____

   Long-term impacts:

_____

_____

_____

5. Looking back at the incident, what could you have done differently to avoid being intimidating, even if you were upset? If you are in a group, ask the group members or your counselor for ideas.

_____

_____

_____

_____

Part 3: Please review the following examples of practicing and assessing one's progress.

1. **Practicing: Making a life-changing plan for being nonthreatening.** If you are currently in a relationship, think of ways you can remain nonthreatening with your partner or your children in the future. If you're not in a relationship, describe ways you will ensure that you won't be threatening or intimidating with a future partner. If you're in a group, ask your counselor or other group members for ideas.

   Be mindful of my voice and talk in a nonthreatening manner. Stay aware of my body language. Take a time-out if I sense that I might become violent or intimidating. Allow her to express herself; don't get agitated or controlling. Practice interacting without using gestures, glares, or raising my voice.

   Note: Leaving without an explanation can be very threatening to a victim. Not knowing when an angry person who has been violent in the past will return can be very scary.

2. **Assessing your progress.** Return to this section of the workbook after several weeks of following your plan. Write down the results of your changed behavior.

   At family get-togethers I put Rena down a lot. I'm not even sure why—maybe so I look better. Everyone laughs and Rena plays along, but I know she's hurt. When she confronts me later, I just say I was teasing. Last time we were all together, I didn't make fun of her. Instead, when I talked about Alex's good grades, I made sure to talk about how much effort Rena puts into our kids' academic achievement. She seemed kind of proud.

Part 4: Please answer the following questions.

1. **Practicing.** If you are currently in a relationship, think of ways you can remain nonthreatening with your partner or your children in the future. If you're not in a relationship, describe ways you will ensure that you won't be threatening or intimidating with a future partner. If you're in a group, ask your counselor or other group members for ideas.

   _____

   _____

   _____

   _____

   _____

   _____

   _____

2. **Assessing your progress.** Return to this section of the workbook after several weeks of following your plan, and write down the results of your changed behavior.

_____

_____

_____

_____

_____

_____

> If you're in a domestic abuse group, discuss this exercise together, preferably in small groups. Each participant should talk about what he learned from the exercise.

A Closing Thought

Boys and young men learn about the power of intimidation from their fathers (and sometimes their mothers), male (and sometimes female) siblings, bullies in their schools and neighborhoods, coaches, the military, and representations in the media. We learn through observation (i.e., by seeing what scares another person) and by practice. Intimidation is both offensive and defensive. The person on the receiving end of the intimidating behavior is immediately put on the defensive, similar to when an unleashed dog confronts you; you're never sure of its next move. Some men claim they need this "male pose" to survive in a violent world, but using threatening behavior in an intimate relationship is simply not conducive to respect or love.

For men who batter, the use of intimidation in intimate relationships is usually calculated. When a couple is having a disagreement, the man may escalate his use of intimidation until his partner acquiesces. His goal is to deflect her anger or to end the argument on his terms. Through his body language, tone of voice, slamming of doors, pounding on tables, and throwing and breaking things, he is able to instill enough fear in his partner that she will usually (but not always) back down. Even if a man is not in an argument, some men will use a pre-emptive strike by acting like they are going to explode at any moment. The message is clear: Don't mess with me. This is frightening and, unfortunately, effective.

I've never met a man who has battered who hasn't used intimidating behaviors in an intimate relationship. Some men have said they like having the power and "respect" in their households and that intimidation is a means to that end. But at what cost? Do you really want your partner and children to be fearful of you? Do you want your family to walk on eggshells whenever you're home? Being nonthreatening might be one of the biggest challenges you face in your change process. It will require practice, patience, new ways of communicating, listening without getting defensive, talking and acting in a calm manner, and being open to feedback from your partner without her fearing retribution.

Being Fair

Sometimes men who batter threaten further violence. Women who have been beaten in the past take these threats seriously, for good reason. Several men in our groups have said that their partners know they wouldn't actually do what they threatened to do, but how can their partners be sure? And if a man has been violent in the past, why wouldn't his partner think the threats were real? Why did her partner make the threats in the first place?

For example, some men threaten to take away or gain custody of the children. They know women feel particularly vulnerable in this area, and they choose to exploit this vulnerability. Other men threaten to harm themselves. Some men physically block the door so their partners can't get into or out of the house. Others threaten to leave or get a divorce. For some battered women the threats and the fear of further violence are paralyzing. As Emma told me during an interview:

> I never involved law enforcement. We lived in an isolated area, so if an incident was taking place, I would have had to walk for a mile to get to a pay phone. I wouldn't leave the girls with him, so I just had to deal with his beatings. He had guns, which he wasn't afraid to use, and there were many nights that he would fire shots to scare me. This was terrifying. He would lock me out of the house in the middle of the night, but I would never leave to get help, because I couldn't stand the thought of leaving the children with him.

Threats and coercion are powerful weapons, especially if you've used violence against your intimate partner in the past. *Can you recall times when you've resorted to using threats and coercion to get your way? Let's examine these behaviors and explore what fairness looks like in an intimate relationship.*

EXERCISE 2 Being Fair

The following exercise is for men who *choose* and *want* to be fair with their intimate partners. The goal is to stop making threats or using coercion against (pressuring) their partners.

Part 1: Please review the following examples of threats and coercion.

Examples of threats

- threatened to leave
- threatened to take all the money
- threatened to expose personal information to her family, friends, or coworkers
- threatened to take the children or get custody of them
- threatened to report her to welfare or child protection services
- threatened to call her probation officer

Examples of pressuring

- forced her to drop charges
- pressured her to give up friendships
- pressured her to do illegal things

Examples of warnings

- told her you'd kill yourself if she left
- told her you'd hurt her, family members, the children, her friends, pets
- told her she would "pay" if she testified in court

Part 2: Please answer the following questions.

1. List several incidents when you used threatening behavior with a past or current partner. Threats can be a means of pressuring, or they can be warnings that something bad will happen to your partner or the children unless she changes or does something you want her to do.

_____

_____

_____

_____

2. Pick the incident from your list that most stands out in your mind. Describe it in detail.

_____

_____

_____

_____

_____

3. What was the purpose of your behavior? Describe what you were feeling and thinking.

_____

_____

_____

_____

4. What were the short-term and long-term impacts of your behavior?
   Short-term impacts:

_____

_____

_____

   Long-term impacts:

_____

_____

_____

5. Looking back at the incident, what could you have done differently to avoid making threats, even if you were angry or felt betrayed? If you are in a group, ask the group members or the counselor for ideas.

_____

_____

_____

_____

Part 3: Please review the following examples of practicing and assessing one's progress.

1. **Practicing: Making a life-changing plan for being fair.** If you are currently in a relationship, think of ways you can stop making threats and commit to being evenhanded with your partner by negotiating in a fair manner. If you're not in a relationship, describe ways you will ensure that you won't be threatening with a future partner.

   Be aware of threatening comments. Accept the legal consequences for my violent behavior, with the knowledge that good things will ultimately happen. If I'm feeling suicidal, I'll get help—I can work through these problems. Recognize that threats will be met by resistance and in the long run won't work. Talk to group members about feelings and issues. Commit to not pressuring her in any way.

2. **Assessing your progress.** Return to this section of the workbook after several weeks of following your plan, and write down the results of your changed behavior.

   We have been at this stalemate over how we are going to use the tax refund. In the past I've made a lot of threatening comments about leaving her with all of the debt we've accumulated. She usually gives in when we argue about money, but she's resentful. I told her that I'd like to work this issue out. We used the Negotiation Guide from the groups. It was a little weird, but it really worked.

   Note: The Negotiation Guide appears on page 118.

Part 4: Please answer the following questions.

1. **Practicing.** If you are currently in a relationship, think of ways you can stop making threats and commit to being evenhanded with your partner by negotiating in a fair manner. If you're not in a relationship, describe ways you will ensure that you won't be threatening with a future partner.

_____

_____

_____

_____

_____

_____

_____

2. **Assessing your progress.** Return to this section of the workbook after several weeks of following your plan, and write down the results of your changed behavior.

_____

_____

_____

_____

_____

_____

> If you're in a domestic abuse group, discuss this exercise together, preferably in small groups. Each participant should talk about what he learned from the exercise. The group can use the Negotiation Guide and Fair Discussion Guide, found in Chapter 8 of this workbook, for specific techniques.

A Closing Thought

Making threats that negative things will happen to your partner if she doesn't change is a form of coercion. Imagine yourself walking into a room and someone telling you that there was a two hundred pound weight above your head. If the person controlling the weight told you to comply with certain orders or the weight would be dropped on your head, what would you do? Of course you'd comply. But how would you feel and what would you think? You'd most likely be scared, anxious, and angry. You'd be constantly thinking about how to get out of such a dangerous situation. You might alter your behavior in order to please the person who had the power to drop the weight on you.

Later in the workbook you will practice exercises that will help you look at problems from both sides of the issue, recognize that there are many ways to resolve conflicts in an equitable manner, learn techniques for compromising, and discover new ways to negotiate in a fair way.

Being Trusting and Supportive

"Isolation" is a term we use in domestic abuse groups. It is generally defined as any attempt to control who your partner sees, what she does, what she wants for herself, what she thinks, or what she feels. A man who batters does this by making demands that his partner end her relationships with certain friends or family members whom he disproves of, or who he thinks are threatening. He may sabotage or pressure his partner to give up activities she enjoys, or place obstacles so she can't fulfill her aspirations. For example, he may not be supportive when his partner wants to apply for a better job, take classes, get involved in a community group or politics, participate in athletics, or go out with friends.

When men who batter try to isolate their intimate partners, it's not just out of jealousy or possessiveness, although these feelings are often very real. Men who batter usually know that their violence has damaged their relationship. They've seen the fear and terror in their partner's eyes. They've witnessed their partner covering her bruises or staunching a wound. You can easily recall the nights of screaming, crying, and rage. Depending on the severity of your violence and how long it has been occurring, your partner is probably filled with resentment. You know on some level that she has contemplated leaving.

She might be staying because she hopes things will change. She may feel partially responsible for what has happened. She may fear being out on her own or feel financially trapped. If you have children together, she may be reluctant to end the relationship. And she might be afraid of you. Any attempt on her part at independence causes you anxiety because you're never certain of her motivation. What are her friends telling her? What is she saying to that counselor or advocate from the battered women's shelter? Why does she want get a new job or to make more money?

Cassie, a woman who had been battered, told me that her partner wanted her to better herself, but only up to a point:

> Antonio encouraged me to go back to school, and I did. But as I got close to graduating from college, he made things very difficult. I don't think he ever thought I'd get to that point, so when I did, he said I was neglecting the house and the kids. It was literally a fight for me to get out the door to attend my classes.
>
> After I graduated, he encouraged me to get a job. He'd say, "You're a smart woman, you've got a degree, and you can get a good job." So I got a job, but I had to start at the bottom. Everything was okay and he was supportive until I started to work my way up the ladder. He got threatened by the people I worked with. And I think he felt inadequate because I was making more money than him. That's when the beatings started getting real bad. I think he felt like less of a man.

Sylvie, who was quoted earlier, stated that her partner cut off her relationships with friends for a specific reason:

> When we first started dating I had a lot of friends, and Tyler seemed okay with that. But things changed, especially when the physical violence intensified. He started to devalue my friends. If a friend of mine gave me clothing as a Christmas present, he would use it as a rag to wash the car. He'd say, "I don't know why you want to hang around her, she ain't no good."
>
> He wanted the power to make me feel bad and to make me feel good. So my having friends was a threat because they could make me feel better, and he wanted to be the only one who could do that.

To repair the damage in an existing relationship or to ensure that you don't try to isolate a partner in the future, it's important to understand why you wanted to control or limit your partner's independence. What were your fears? Did this kind of controlling behavior begin right away in your relationship, or did it happen when you started using violence? *Remember the times when you've used isolation to control your intimate partner. How can you be trusting and supportive in the future?*

Being Trusting and Supportive

The following exercise is for men who *choose* and *want* to trust and support their intimate partners. The goal is to stop blocking their partner's freedom to make decisions. Think carefully about each part of the exercise.

> Before beginning make sure you're in a quiet place where you won't be interrupted. Take some deep breaths to relax and clear your mind.

Part 1: Please review the following examples of isolating behaviors.

Examples of checking up on her

- made her tell me what she did and who she talked to
- listened to her phone conversations
- looked at her text messages, e-mails, or phone messages
- accused her of doing things behind my back
- called her workplace, friends, and family to monitor her activities
- questioned her when she came home
- demanded to know where she'd been when she was late

Examples of trying to stop her from doing something

- discouraged her from going to school
- tried to persuade her not to change jobs or accept a promotion
- got jealous when she worked late or spent time with work friends
- sabotaged her involvement in community groups, counseling, and women's groups
- went to her workplace when I wasn't expected

Examples of interfering with her social life

- made it difficult for her to have friends I didn't approve of
- wouldn't let her have male friends
- wouldn't let her go to parties or functions without me
- acted jealous in public and in private
- accused her of having affairs or flirting
- undermined family social activities

- got into fights before a social activity so she'd be too upset to go
- wouldn't take care of the children so she couldn't leave
- disabled her car
- took her cell phone
- purposely moved our household to an isolated area

Part 2: Please answer the following questions.

1. List several incidents when you have used isolating behavior with a past or current partner.

_____

_____

_____

2. Pick the incident from your list that most stands out in your mind. Describe it in detail. (Include checking up her, trying to stop her from doing something, or interfering with her social life.)

_____

_____

_____

_____

_____

3. What was the purpose of your behavior? Describe what you were feeling and thinking.

_____

_____

_____

4. What were the short-term and long-term impacts of your behavior?
   Short-term impacts:

_____

_____

_____

Long-term impacts:

_____

_____

_____

5. Looking back at the incident, what could you have done differently to avoid controlling or isolating your partner, even though you might have felt jealous, insecure, or thought you were right? (If you are in a group, ask other group members or the counselor for ideas.)

_____

_____

_____

_____

_____

_____

_____

Part 3: Review the following examples of practicing and assessing one's progress.

1. **Practicing: Making a life-changing plan for being trusting and supportive.** If you are currently in a relationship, think of ways you can stop isolating your partner and commit to trusting and supporting her. If you're not in a relationship, describe ways you will ensure that you won't attempt to isolate a future partner.

   Support her goals; respect her right to choose her own friends; avoid sabotaging her plans; keep negative thoughts about her choices to myself; talk with group members or my counselor about feelings of jealousy; avoid undermining social events, checking up on her, or trying to control her life.

2. **Assessing your progress.** Return to this section of the workbook after several weeks of following your plan, and write down the results of your changed behavior.

   On the way home I asked her some questions about her day at work. Later I asked her about a problem she was having with her boss. I'm usually disinterested in her job, so I don't communicate much. When she started talking, I really listened. I understood some of the stress she was feeling. I really do want to be more supportive, and I know she wants that.

Part 4: Please answer the following questions.

1. **Practicing.** If you are currently in a relationship, think of ways you can stop isolating your partner and commit to trusting and supporting her. If you're not in a relationship, describe ways you will ensure that you won't attempt to isolate a future partner.

_____

_____

_____

_____

_____

2. **Assessing your progress.** Return to this section of the workbook after several weeks of following your plan, and write down the results of your changed behavior.

_____

_____

_____

_____

_____

> If you're in a domestic abuse group, discuss this exercise together, preferably in small groups. Each participant should talk about what he learned from the exercise.

A Closing Thought

Even in relationships where there hasn't been domestic abuse, men and women can feel insecure or even jealous about the relationship. This can happen when communication breaks down, disagreements remain unsettled, or intimacy wanes. Couples lead busy lives, and they sometimes don't take the time to connect or talk through their problems. When this happens partners can grow distant, and you might be unsure how to get back to a good place.

If you've been violent with your partner, as you know by now, everything changes. If you're committed to making your present relationship work, your partner will want and expect you to trust her and be supportive. But she needs to believe that you're really changing. Too many men in our domestic abuse groups know what to say, but their actions don't match their words. Some men will be on their "best behavior" for a short time to appease their partners and then revert back to familiar territory—and the destructive patterns start all over again.

Even if your relationship improves, sometimes change can be upsetting. You don't know what to expect, and the uncertainty can be unnerving. Your partner deserves to have her own life, and both of you need space to grow independently of each other. When that happens and trust is reestablished, you can support each other's goals and aspirations because your union will be based on love and concern for each other's happiness. This may take time, but make the commitment now.

Being a Caring Father

If you have children, they very likely have been exposed to your violence. At some point you may want to find ways to repair your relationship with them. When you're ready for this conversation, remember that they might not be. Their experiences (witnessing your violence and other abusive behavior) may be too fresh and painful. You may need help from a counselor.

If you talk to your children, be honest. Trying to justify or rationalize your actions will not be helpful. Explain that what occurred in the past was your responsibility and yours alone. Reassure them that they are not at fault. Let them know that you are taking steps to change.

As Dave said in the book *Violent No More*:

> For a while [my son] was having problems with his girlfriend. I talked with him a lot about the choices we make and being respectful in relationships. We've talked about what he saw growing up—me hitting his mother. He understands how it might have affected him, and he can see that he's being abusive, even though he hasn't hurt his girlfriend physically. I try to use my life and the things I did wrong as a way for my kids to learn. I do what I can to help them. I wish I could erase what happened in the past, but I can't. I can only be there for them now.

Some men who batter use their children as weapons against their current or former partners. A man who batters may belittle or undermine his partner in front of the children. He may threaten to take the children away or threaten to gain custody by claiming that his partner is an unfit mother. For couples who are separated, some men attempt to manipulate or interrogate their children to get information about their former partners.

Divorce can bring out the worst in some couples, especially when children are involved. When there has been domestic abuse, there is often an added dimension. Far too many men who batter will acknowledge (after they've completed a domestic abuse group and recognized all the ways they were abusive) that they used the children to get back at their partners.

Not all men who have battered use their children, and many are devoted fathers. Yet all too often, because of the bitterness of a failed relationship or as a tactic to get what they want, some men who batter make custody threats. Some do it under the guise of love for their children, and others base it on their rights as fathers.

It doesn't have to be like this. Your children may have already experienced trauma because of the violence in the home, and compounding those events with acrimony stemming from your separation or divorce isn't helpful. *Remember the times when you've used your children to control your intimate partner. How can you become a more caring father?*

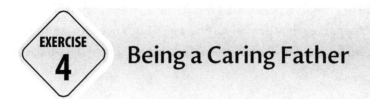

Being a Caring Father

EXERCISE 4

The following exercise is for men who *choose* and *want* to be caring fathers. The goal is to stop using the children as a way to get back at their partners or former partners. It will also help men commit to being better dads. Think carefully about each step of the exercise, and write down your responses. If you don't have children, review the exercise anyway, even if you don't complete the questions. You could have children or stepchildren in the future, or you might have memories from your own childhood. After reviewing the exercise, move on to the next exercise.

> Before beginning make sure you're in a quiet place where you won't be interrupted. Take some deep breaths to relax and clear your mind.

Part 1: Please review the following examples of how some men who have battered used their children against their partners or ex-partners.

Examples of making your partner feel guilty

- told her she was a bad, unfit, or incompetent mother
- threatened to report her to child protective services
- compared her to other women who I think have better parenting skills

Examples of using the children

- told the children that their mother is bad, amoral, or the reason the relationship ended
- used the children to relay messages to their mother
- tried to obtain information from the children about their mother's activities, especially when she was dating
- told the children they couldn't do something they wanted to do because of their mother

Examples of making threats

- threatened to get custody
- threatened to take the children and leave the state
- threatened to harm the children

Examples of abuse in front of the children

- was violent, threatening, or intimidating while the children were present
- called her names and put her down while the children were in the house
- criticized her parenting skills in front of the children

Part 2: Please answer the following questions.

1. List several incidents when you used the children to get back at a past or current partner, or incidents when you were abusive or made threats to your partner while the children were present.

_____

_____

_____

_____

_____

2. Pick the incident from your list that most stands out in your mind. Describe it in detail. (For example, making your partner feel guilty, using the children, making threats that involve the children, or being abusive in front of the children.)

_____

_____

_____

_____

_____

3. What was the purpose of your behavior? Describe what you were feeling and thinking.

_____

_____

_____

4. What were the short-term and long-term impacts of your behavior?
Short-term impacts:

_____

_____

Long-term impacts:

_____

_____

5. Looking back at the incident, what could you have done differently to avoid involving the children, even if you were angry with your partner or former partner? (If you are in a group, ask the group members or the counselor for ideas.)

_____

_____

_____

Part 3: Please review the following examples of practicing and assessing one's progress.

1. **Practicing: Making a life-changing plan for being a caring father.** If you are currently in a relationship and have children, think of ways you can be a more responsible parent. In the future, how will you ensure that you don't use the children against your partner or ex-partner?

   I'll avoid arguing when the children are present. I won't tell the children negative things about their mother. I won't start a fight or harass their mother when I'm picking up or dropping off the children from visitation. I'll be a positive role model, do more things with the kids, spend quality time with them, and share parental responsibilities with their mother.

2. **Assessing your progress.** Return to this section of the workbook after several weeks of following your plan, and write down the results of your changed behavior.

   I started thinking about all the excuses I had made about not having time to spend with my kids. I asked Sean and Libby if they wanted to go on a bike ride, and they were super happy. I want them to know that I do love them and I am changing. It wasn't much, but I felt better.

Part 4: Please answer the following questions.

1. **Practicing.** If you are currently in a relationship and have children, think of ways you can be a more responsible parent. In the future, how will you ensure that you don't use the children against your partner or ex-partner?

_____

_____

_____

_____

_____

2. **Assessing your progress.** Return to this section of the workbook after several weeks of following your plan, and write down the results of your changed behavior.

_____

_____

_____

Note: If you are separated or divorced and have children, review the chart on the following page, which was created by the Domestic Abuse Intervention Project Father's Nonviolence Program.

- Can you commit to the topics you can/should discuss?
- Can you commit to the topics not to discuss?
- Does this fit with your life-changing plan for being a caring father?

> If you're in a domestic abuse group, discuss this exercise together, preferably in small groups. Each participant should talk about what he learned from the exercise.

A Closing Thought

In our domestic abuse groups, the issue of child custody can lead to explosive emotions. Many participants who have children believe that the court system is unfair to men. This is a complex issue. On the one hand, I'm pleased that more fathers want to take a more active role in their children's lives. On the other hand, the court has to think about what's in the best interest of the children when considering custody. If there's been domestic abuse, that is a factor the court should consider.

Keep your issues with your ex-partner separate—and away—from your children. Be involved in their lives. Encourage them to grow, learn, and be productive citizens. Be supportive and help them resolve problems.

Many men who go through their change process are remorseful as they begin to recognize how their domestic abuse affected not only their partners but also their children. You have an opportunity to make amends with your children and also to demonstrate that people can change. Although statistics show that children who are exposed to domestic abuse are at greater risk of becoming abusive as adults, this doesn't mean that children who witnessed domestic abuse are automatically condemned to be abusers. Your children may need help from a counselor, and they may persevere on their own. Being a caring and loving father who shows genuine integrity in his future actions can be a powerful example.

DAIP Father's Nonviolence Program
Parenting After Separation

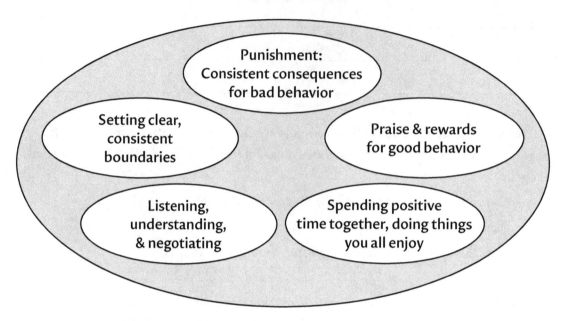

1. **Do not be afraid to talk about scary events.** Don't bring them up yourself, but if the child brings one up, listen, answer, provide comfort and support.

2. **Provide a consistent, predictable pattern for the day.** Explain beforehand what's going to happen, explain what's different and why, stay calm.

3. **Be nurturing, comforting, and affectionate.** Offer hugs and comfort when children want it. Don't demand affection, but return it when it's offered.

4. **Discuss what you expect for behavior and your style of discipline.** Avoid physical discipline, reward positive behavior. Provide consistent but flexible rules and consequences.

5. **Talk with your child.** Offer information that suits their age; tell the truth, admit it if you don't know the answer.

6. **Protect the child.** Avoid or limit activities that upset them.

7. **Give children choices and some sense of control.** Offer ways to do things that encourage maturity.

8. **If you have questions, ask for help.** The more informed you are, the better you can help your children.

Topics not to discuss

- Arrangements for child support

- Anger, resentment, frustration with their mother or her family

- Questions about who their mother is seeing, where she lives, where she works—anything NOT related to your child's regular activities

- Any feelings you have for their mother outside the parenting relationship

- Your feelings about her new partner

Topics you can/should discuss

- When and where you will see them next

- Anything positive about their mother as a parent or her family

- Your child's feelings about the separation or divorce

- That problems between you and their mother are not their fault

- That you love them no matter what

Being Respectful

Emotional abuse may not be illegal, but many battered women report that the degrading comments, humiliating experiences, and name calling were as painful as the physical blows they endured. What made it all worse, they often say, was that they knew their partners were intentionally trying to hurt or embarrass them. They were profoundly affected by their partners' purposeful attempts to degrade and humiliate them. When they learned more about battering, they understood that the emotional abuse was a strategy used by their partner to keep them down by damaging their spirits and self-esteem.

Objectification of groups of people is a major weapon of those who want to dominate others. Think of all the cruel names and dehumanizing comments that white people in this country used against people of color to justify slavery, segregation, and genocide. Consider the following analogy. European settlers and explorers came to the Americas about five hundred years ago. They sought to exploit natural resources and claim the land for their use; however, they encountered indigenous people who had been on the continent for thousands of years. The church at that time believed and taught that all non-Christians were savages and heathens. Consequently the explorers believed they had God on their side as they sought to take over the new land by dispossessing the indigenous people. In order to oppress, the oppressor needs to dehumanize the person or persons he is oppressing, which is precisely what the invading Europeans did. They saw the indigenous people as defective because they did not embrace European culture and religion. Persecution was then easily justified.

Notice the parallels between the European view of indigenous people and the beliefs some men hold about women. Men who batter often use vile names for their partners prior to an assault. Calling them "bitch" or "cunt" makes them less than human. As Sylvie told me, emotional abuse usually accompanied her partner's physical violence:

> I hated being called a bitch. I'd tell him, "I'm not a bitch; a bitch is a female dog." One time during a bad assault he made me get down on all fours. He said, "See, you are a bitch." He never totally broke my spirit despite the things he said and did, though if I'd stayed with him, he probably would have.

Another woman, Cassie, told me she started believing the things her partner was saying:

> Antonio told me I was ignorant and incompetent. When I first got my job, I thought these people who hired me must not realize I'm incompetent. And when he would tell me that no judge would give me custody of the children because I was a bad mother, I believed him.
>
> When we were intimate, I would tell him personal things. But I was always sorry I did because he would use them against me. It was almost like he was recording them and just waiting for the right time to bring them up. When he called me names, it made me feel like I wasn't even human.

Emotional abuse can take on many shapes and forms. Some people in intimate relationships withhold their thoughts or feelings, use the "silent treatment," or refuse to engage their partners. If a man has battered, his partner may be reluctant to challenge his silence because she has experienced the flip side of this behavior. Some men in our groups don't realize, or choose not to acknowledge, how painful it can be to be on the receiving end of criticism, sarcasm, or judgmentalism. They defensively claim that their partners are overly sensitive, can't take a joke, or are blowing a remark way out of proportion. They see themselves in a no-win situation and as the "real" victims. If being judgmental or using sarcasm is part of the emotional abuse arsenal of a man who batters, the words, regardless of the intent, chip away at his partner's self-confidence.

As was stated in the book *Violent No More,* both men and women can be emotionally abusive. Even in the healthiest relationships, people occasionally say hurtful things. Usually when we do this we're reacting defensively to feeling hurt ourselves; one partner may inadvertently say something hurtful, and the other responds in kind. However, in healthy relationships, partners usually don't make hurtful or shaming comments on purpose, and if it does happen, the person who made the comment often concedes that the put-down or remark was wrong. There's usually some accountability, an honest explanation, and an apology for what was said. The confrontation may have been painful, but it probably wasn't destructive.

Being respectful in an intimate relationship sounds like an easy goal. But for many men who batter, it can be a struggle. Men who have been habitually disrespectful, possessively jealous, combative, and controlling often find communicating respectfully (at least on a consistent basis) difficult. One man in our group stated that he had been sarcastic and impolite for so long in his relationship with his wife that being nice seemed almost foreign. Genuinely communicating in a respectful manner is a choice. In later chapters there are exercises to help you reach this goal. For now, *remember the times when you have been emotionally abusive with your intimate partner. How can you be respectful in the future?*

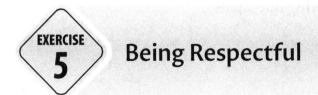

EXERCISE 5

Being Respectful

The following exercise is for men who *choose* and *want* to be respectful in their relationships with their intimate partners. The goal is to stop being emotionally abusive. Think carefully about each part of the exercise before writing your responses.

> Before beginning make sure you're in a quiet place where you won't be interrupted. Take some deep breaths to relax and clear your mind.

Part 1: Please review the following examples of emotional abuse.

Examples of name calling

- called her derogatory names with sexual connotations (slut, cunt, whore, etc.)
- called her names that made her feel bad about her body (ugly, fat, etc.)

Examples of put-downs

- told her she was stupid, incompetent, lazy, a bad mother, a bad lover
- belittled her by saying, "I must have been crazy to marry you" or "Can't you do anything right?" or "Nobody else would want you"
- humiliated her in front of the children, friends, coworkers, family

Examples of making her feel guilty and degrading her

- blamed her when the kids did something wrong
- blamed her for financial problems
- blamed her when the sex wasn't good; made accusations and disparaging comments about her body and her lovemaking ability
- threw food at her
- played mind games; insinuated that she's mentally ill or that something is wrong with her

Part 2: Please answer the following questions.

1. List several incidents when you were emotionally abusive with a past or current partner.

_____

_____

_____

_____

_____

2. Pick the incident from your list that most stands out in your mind. Describe it in detail (e.g., name calling, put-downs, making your partner feel guilty, degrading her).

_____

_____

_____

_____

_____

3. What was the purpose of your behavior? Describe what you were feeling and thinking.

_____

_____

_____

4. What were the short-term and long-term impacts of your behavior?
   Short-term impacts:

_____

_____

   Long-term impacts:

_____

_____

_____

5. Looking back at the incident, what could you have done differently to avoid being emotionally abusive, even if you were angry, defensive, hurt, or felt rejected in some way? (If you are in a group, ask the group members or counselor for ideas.)

_____

_____

_____

Part 3: Please review the following examples of practicing and assessing one's progress.

1. **Practicing: Making a life-changing plan for being respectful.** If you are currently in a relationship, think of ways you can stop using emotional abuse and commit to being respectful with your intimate partner. If you're not in a relationship, describe ways you will ensure that you won't be emotionally abusive with a future partner.

   If I'm angry at her, I won't call her names or use put-downs. I will listen to her in a nonjudgmental manner. I won't blame or criticize her if things go wrong or if she makes a mistake. I will use positive self-talk and take time-outs when I'm agitated or angry. I will talk to my fellow group members and counselor about my plan to eliminate emotional abuse in my relationship.

   Note: The Time-Out Rules are listed on page 103.

2. **Assessing your progress.** Return to this section of the workbook after several weeks of following your plan, and write down the results of your changed behavior.

   The last time we had an argument, I remained calm and really listened to her side. I could tell she seemed more relaxed because I wasn't going off on her and I was respectful. I actually felt better about myself.

Part 4: Please answer the following questions.

1. **Practicing.** If you are currently in a relationship, think of ways you can stop using emotional abuse and commit to being respectful with your intimate partner. If you're not in a relationship, describe ways you will ensure that you won't be emotionally abusive with a future partner.

_____

_____

_____

_____

2. **Assessing your progress.** Return to this section of the workbook after several weeks of following your plan, and write down the results of your changed behavior.

_____

_____

_____

_____

> If you're in a domestic abuse group, discuss this exercise together, preferably in small groups. Each participant should talk about what he learned from the exercise.

A Closing Thought

Some men might feel that this section on emotional abuse is unfair. They will point to numerous occasions when their partners have put them down, humiliated them publicly, or called them names. I don't deny that this happens or condone the behavior. For some battered women, fighting back verbally may provide some semblance of resistance when they're being slapped, kicked, or dragged around the room by their hair. Many battered women will physically fight back and, when unsuccessful, will try to even the score by being emotionally abusive. It's natural for people who are victimized to resist.

If you are hoping to reestablish the relationship with the woman you battered, you know that a lot has to change. At some point, when you've completed your domestic abuse group and your partner feels safe, you may want to consider marriage counseling so both of you can find practical tools to be respectful to one another. This will take a strong commitment. I've seen couples make incredible changes, but it must start with you. If you don't believe in equality between men and women, if you don't support your partner's aspirations, if you don't trust your partner, or if you're not willing to compromise, marriage counseling will be of little help. You've come a long way, so please continue working.

Understanding and Stopping Battering

As you know from reading the book *Violent No More* and using this workbook, domestic abuse is more than physical and sexual violence. As stated earlier, the Power and Control Wheel, shown at the beginning of the chapter, was created by the Domestic Abuse Intervention Project to illustrate the abusive behaviors used by men who batter to silence, scare, manipulate, confuse, and control their partners. Take a few minutes to look once again at the Power and Control Wheel on page 38 before completing Exercise 6.

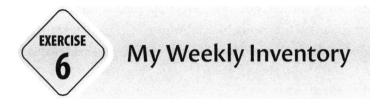

My Weekly Inventory

If you are currently in an intimate relationship, take an honest inventory on a weekly basis to monitor how you may still be using abusive behavior. Refer to the Power and Control Wheel as well as the lists you've generated from the exercises you've completed. Make twenty-six copies of this page so you can complete your weekly inventory for six months. (If you are in a counseling or domestic abuse program, they might be able to provide you with enough copies of the weekly inventory.) If you're not currently in a relationship, go to the next chapter in the workbook, but if you get into an intimate partnership in the future, it would be a good idea to return to this exercise and complete the weekly inventory for six months.

> Before beginning make sure you're in a quiet place where you won't be interrupted. Take some deep breaths to relax and clear your mind.

Part 1: Please answer the following questions.

1. List any abusive behaviors that you used in the past week.

_____

_____

_____

2. What was the purpose of your behavior?

_____

_____

_____

3. How could you have handled the situation differently?

_____

_____

_____

4. If you stopped yourself from using violence or other abusive behaviors during the past week, describe why and how you made the choice to handle the situation differently. Did you use any of the exercises or guides in this workbook to help you? If yes, please explain.

_____

_____

_____

> **If you're in a domestic abuse group, discuss this exercise together, preferably in small groups. Each participant should talk about what he learned from the exercise.**

A Closing Thought

If you are in an intimate relationship, pay close attention to your reactions to your partner, especially when you have disagreements. Catch and stop yourself every time you start using abusive behavior to hurt, control, or punish your partner. Even if you're angry, step back and think about how you're going to respond. Seek constructive alternatives. Self-control and making positive decisions to avoid being abusive are possible, but only if you have self-awareness and *choose* alternative behaviors.

Remaining nonviolent must occur over a sustained period of time, which is why I advise using this weekly inventory while you're in your domestic abuse program and even after completing it. In our domestic abuse groups, men often report on the positive progress they are making. When they complete the weekly inventory, they acknowledge their abusive behavior, even if it didn't rise to the level of using physical violence, intimidation, threats, or coercion. They recognize that they had alternatives to being abusive and often feel affirmed for the way they responded. Maybe their response wasn't perfect, but they didn't use violence and didn't make their partner fearful. All too often, if men are not monitoring their reactions to conflicts and problems, some of them will revert to their old ways when an event occurs or an issue arises. Even if you think you'll never batter again, keep monitoring your behavior. It will keep you on your path.

Getting Past Denial

When people break the rules or policies at work they usually try to justify their actions—their jobs may depend on it. When parents have their parenting skills challenged, they may maintain that they did the best job they could—their sense of integrity may depend on it. When someone has an affair, he or she may straight out lie—their relationship or reputation may depend on it.

Back in 1964 Kitty Genovese was stabbed to death by an attacker in New York City. As she was being stabbed in the back, she screamed, "Oh my god, he stabbed me! Help me!" It was revealed that there were thirty-eight witnesses to the crime, most of whom heard her screams for help. Apparently none of the neighbors did anything to help. What we define as the "bystander effect" led to the silence. People questioned how law-abiding citizens refused to get involved. Similarly, atrocities have been committed in war as civilian and military personnel have remained silent. People either feared questioning authority or were afraid for their own safety.

> *When you think everything is someone else's fault, you will suffer a lot. When you realize that everything springs only from yourself, you will learn both peace and joy.*
>
> — THE FOURTEENTH DALAI LAMA

We all have what might be considered ethical or moral lapses. We hope we'll do the right things regardless of the consequences, but that's not always the case.

When people get arrested for criminal behavior, they respond in different ways. If someone is caught red-handed, they might be resigned to their fate and accept responsibility for their deeds. For some people the decision to plead not guilty is based on a strategy: They hope a good lawyer will get them a reduced sentence in a plea agreement.

Beyond the legal consequences of wrongdoing (going to jail or prison and paying fines), most people have a hard time accepting responsibility for their behavior. When stopped for speeding, how many people say, "Sorry, officer, I was in a hurry. Write me a ticket." Not many. People usually say, "I couldn't have been speeding." "There must be something wrong with my speedometer." "I didn't see the speed limit sign." "My wife was in a terrible accident and I have to get to the hospital." Police officers have heard all of the excuses.

When a corporate CEO or a person in a position of power is implicated in corruption, the first thing out of their mouth (or their lawyer's) is usually, "I'm confident that when all the facts are in, I'll be fully exonerated."

Richard Nixon, the thirty-seventh president of the United States, repeatedly denied being involved in clandestine and illegal activities during his presidency. The Watergate scandal dominated the country for two years until the House Judiciary Committee opened impeachment hearings. Nixon finally resigned in 1974, even though he maintained that he hadn't committed any crimes. Years later he would say things like, "I let my country down," but he never fully accepted responsibility for Watergate and the related criminal behavior.

Bill Clinton, the forty-second president of the United States, was impeached by the House of Representatives for alleged acts of perjury and obstruction of justice in the Monica Lewinski scandal. On national television Clinton said, "I did not have sexual relations with that woman, Miss Lewinsky." In grand jury testimony he argued, "It depends on what the meaning of the word 'is' is." Years later, Clinton stated that he'd made "a terrible moral error."

When people commit crimes or do something unethical, they usually know that what they are doing is wrong or illegal. They don't expect to get caught. If they can continue committing crimes or behaving unethically without consequences, they may become emboldened: Why stop now? People continue to steal, commit fraud, exploit others, sell harmful drugs, drive under the influence of alcohol, commit incest, rape, cheat, hurt others, and be dishonest until they are stopped. Some people (on their own) become troubled by their dishonorable or illegal behavior and stop. But usually wrongdoers aren't held accountable unless and until the behavior is exposed.

People who are arrested for domestic abuse often deny their actions until they see police reports, pictures of the injuries, and victim and witness statements, and their lawyers explain the legal situation and their chances of getting off.

Domestic violence wasn't always a crime. When it became criminal to assault an intimate partner, neighbors, family members, and law enforcement rarely intervened in what was considered a private matter in the home. When domestic violence became more publicized, it was considered something that happened in "certain households" and to "those people." When laws were enforced more uniformly, offenders were stunned when they were arrested. Although some men accepted responsibility, most denied and minimized their behavior and blamed their partners. They were angry at the police and thought the courts were biased against men. This reaction and attitude hasn't changed over the years. As Ron, a man in our groups, said:

> Jess was afraid of me right from the beginning. I would scream in her face and terrorize her. We would usually fight over little things, but when I wanted the upper hand I would punch holes in the walls or slam things around the house to scare her. One time I put her over my knee and gave her a spanking. This wasn't just a spanking; it was a beating. I was stone-cold sober when I did that to her. I thought of Jess as almost childlike, and if she fucked with me, she was going to get it.
>
> I would usually apologize after I assaulted her, and then I would tell her how much I loved her. During my apologies I'd minimize the incident and blame her for getting me so upset. It was really easy for me to turn things around and then say to her, "You're lucky I don't leave you."

Most men who batter have a hard time getting beyond the rationalization that their violence would not have happened if their partners had simply acted differently. They defend their behavior by stating that the violence was a logical reaction to being provoked. They find it difficult to see any alternative to what they did. *Let's look at some examples of minimizing and blaming.*

Examples of minimizing

When explaining your violence to others you may have heard yourself making minimizing comments like these:

- "It wasn't that bad."
- "I only hit her once."
- "I only slapped her."
- "I would never punch her with a closed fist."
- "She bruises easily."
- "I didn't hit her that hard."
- "I was drunk."
- "This is the first time I've ever done something like that."
- "I just lost it."

Examples of blaming

You may have made blaming statements like these:

- "If she had stopped bitching, I wouldn't have slapped her."
- "If she hadn't come home late, we wouldn't have gotten into it."
- "If she hadn't put me down, I wouldn't have become so upset."
- "If she were a better mother, we wouldn't have these fights."
- "If she didn't drink so much, I wouldn't have hit her."
- "She hit me. What was I supposed to do?"
- "If she didn't come on to other men, I wouldn't have gotten so jealous."

Do these blaming and minimizing statements sound familiar? Let's examine why we minimize and blame others for our actions.

EXERCISE 1 — Why We Minimize and Blame

> Before beginning make sure you're in a quiet place where you won't be interrupted. Take some deep breaths to relax and clear your mind.

Part 1: Please answer the following questions.

1. Close your eyes and think back to a time when you were violent or abusive to someone. This might be your partner, former partner, child, friend, coworker, etc. Remember the incident in great detail. Describe it below.

_____

_____

_____

_____

_____

2. What was it about the situation that made you angry, hurt, or resentful? Explain what you did and what you said to the other person.

_____

_____

_____

3. After the incident, who did you talk to about what happened? If you didn't talk to anyone, you probably thought about what you did. How did you explain the incident to other people or to yourself?

_____

_____

_____

4. How did you justify what you did or said? Did you blame the other person? Did you downplay your actions?

_____

_____

_____

5. Now try to re-create the scene in your mind. Given the same set of circumstances, can you picture yourself handling the situation differently and without being abusive? Are you feeling resistant to imagining yourself handling the situation differently?

_____

_____

_____

> If you're in a domestic abuse group, discuss this exercise together, preferably in small groups. Each participant should talk about what he learned from the exercise.

A Closing Thought

Minimizing what happened and blaming your partner may make it easier for you to justify what you have done. You may feel slightly better about yourself when you explain your violence in a way that makes it seem like you didn't have any other options. You may even get people to sympathize (friends, family members, coworkers, the guys at the bar) with what you did, especially when you tell your story in a certain way. But minimizing and blaming only make it harder to accept responsibility, learn from your mistakes, and change.

Most people feel resistance when they are confronted with an episode in which they were abusive to an intimate partner. Even after many years they can't imagine handling the situation differently. They can still feel the same anger when they replay the unpleasant incident in their mind. Hopefully through your change process you will become open to seeing the bigger picture. In any relationship both parties share responsibility for disagreements and conflicts. But in most cases (unless someone is acting in self-defense or on the rare occasion when there is mutual violence) only one party is responsible for crossing the line and using violence. Getting past denial is an important step you have to take.

Letting Go of Relationships

I'm not a Buddhist, but I've always been attracted to the concepts of mindfulness and being in the moment. I wish I practiced them more. I've also been attracted to the idea that we shouldn't stay attached to things, jobs, or relationships that don't make us happy. I once stayed at a job where I was miserable, in part because I needed the money but also because it provided a perverse sense of security. The longer I stayed, the more the "security" felt like a ball and chain around my ankle. When I finally left I experienced an immediate sense of serenity.

> *Some of us think holding on makes us strong; but sometimes it's letting go.*
>
> — HERMANN HESSE

Attachment is powerful. In intimate relationships it's easy to become emotionally dependent on our partners. This can be good and bad. We get attracted to someone and start relationships in different ways and for varied reasons. Some couples fall passionately in love and quickly move in together or get married. Others take more time to get to know one another, become friends, and chart out a future.

Some couples stay together for a lifetime, but the reality is that many relationships end. I don't use the word "fail" because I don't consider ending a relationship a failure. Life and relationships are complex, and people change. Some couples stay in relationships too long. They don't leave because of the children, because they are financially dependent, because they hope the relationship will improve, because they are afraid of starting over, or because they fear loneliness. Others leave a relationship prematurely and don't make the effort to try to work through problems.

If you're in a domestic abuse group and you know that your relationship ended because of your abusive behavior, you can take the essential steps to learn and change. The exercises in this workbook can help you recognize that while in one sense the violence "worked" (you stopped an argument on your terms or got your way), your ongoing behavior was probably the key factor in driving your partner away. The purpose of the work you're engaged in now is not intended to be shaming, even though you might feel ashamed. It will be hard not to think about the past or to dismiss the negative feelings you have.

The next three exercises deal with strategies to help you to think more positively about your life and your relationship, how to reject jealousy and possessiveness, and, if your relationship ends, how to cope with letting go. *Let's examine some of these ideas and tools that might help you in your current or future relationship.*

Self-Talk and Learning to Think Positively

We've all had experiences with disruptions in our thought process. You might be reading, watching television, working, or talking to somebody, and seemingly out of nowhere, unrelated thoughts enter your mind. This is a distraction, but it's the way our minds work. In yoga practice I try to concentrate on my breathing, and I work at willing away thoughts. As hard as I try, invariably I'm consumed with memories, unresolved issues, and concerns about the day.

As I wrote in the book *Violent No More,* if you feel anxious, jealous, insecure, or angry, you are usually thinking negatively about a situation or a person. Maybe things in your life seem hopeless. You start having negative thoughts: "I'll never get that job; I just don't have the skills." "She doesn't really care about me; I'm wasting my time." "I'm no good; everything I do comes out badly." "I'll never be happy; I might as well stop trying." If you continue to focus on negative thoughts, life feels hopeless. You can also become seriously depressed. You may start taking out your negative thoughts and feelings on others, especially family members. Negativity can become the norm. When this happens, you may stop seeking alternatives that could make you happier and more secure.

The use of positive self-talk is a process of replacing negative messages with positive ones, or at least neutral ones, if overtly positive messages seem too far out of reach at the moment: "I am a good person." "I know I'll succeed if I keep trying." "I have no reason to be jealous." "This problem—like other problems—will pass." You may need to repeat the positive statements many times to erase the negative thoughts. Learning to use positive self-talk, like most changes, takes time, willpower, and concentration.

When negative thoughts creep into your mind, use your positive messages to push the negative ones out the door. It helps greatly to use positive self-talk when you are alone and dwelling on an incident that has upset you. When you're feeling worked up, try taking a long walk by yourself, or even better with a supportive friend. Take long, deep breaths, and repeat the positive self-talk statements from your list. You can even do this on the bus, in the car, or while running or working out. If your counselor in your domestic abuse program recommends that you take a time-out when you think you may become abusive, practice positive self-talk during the time-out. *Self-talk really works. Let's practice.*

Part 1: Please review the following examples of self-talk.

Examples of negative self-talk

- Whenever my partner goes out with her friends, I get jealous.
- There are these two women in particular whom I don't care for, so when she's with them I think the worst.
- When she gets phone messages, I wonder who is texting or calling.
- When men smile or look at her, it makes me suspicious.

Examples of positive self-talk

- I want my wife to have her own friends and her own life.
- I know my girlfriend is attractive, and I have no reason to be jealous.
- People text and call their friends, relatives, and associates, and I need to trust my partner. If there are problems in the relationship, I need to have faith that she will tell me.
- I have to give her time. I just started in this domestic abuse group, and I can't expect that everything will instantly change.

Part 2: Please answer the following questions.

1. Describe an issue or situation with your current or former partner when you were/are preoccupied with negative self-talk.

_____

_____

_____

_____

_____

2. Write down examples of positive self-talk you could have used or can use to counter the negative self-talk.

_____

_____

_____

_____

_____

In addition to doing the above exercise, think about the following (a passage from the book *Violent No More*) when negative self-talk is consuming your mind:

Things will pass: Think of a past situation when you either made a mistake or experienced negative consequences for something you did. Maybe you screwed up big time—made a mistake at work, did something embarrassing at a party, said something to someone that you later regretted. Without excusing what you did, think about how that past negative situation, over time, became less significant. Time does heal. Hopefully you learned something about yourself and won't repeat a similar mistake. *When you're mired in negative self-talk, flip the thought switch that is telling you things won't change. Switch it to a positive thought: Things will change, this will pass, I'll get through this.*

Building empathy: Being responsible for your abusive behavior is hard. You've hurt someone physically or emotionally. We all cling to rationalizations for the bad or inappropriate things we've done, but if you genuinely take responsibility for your actions, you can learn from your mistakes and move on. When I've had a disagreement with my partner, I find that I need to listen to what she is saying on a deeper level. For instance, if my partner tells me that what I did or said was hurtful to her, I may need some time to reflect. This isn't avoidance, but it stops me from being defensive in the moment. I use this time to think about what my partner said. I find it helpful to think about how I would react if the situation were reversed. In other words, how would I feel if my partner said something that I felt was disrespectful of me or my values, even if the comment was unintended? This can be powerful. *If you screwed up, acknowledge it and learn from the experience. We are all imperfect, but we can change.*

> If you're in a domestic abuse group, discuss this exercise together, preferably in small groups. Each participant should talk about what he learned from the exercise.

A Closing Thought

If negative thoughts consistently invade our minds, it influences our mood, motivation, and how we interact with others. Our perceptions of ourselves and our self-concept have been formed from childhood and adult experiences, but we don't have to be trapped in negativity despite setbacks. You can change the way you think about yourself. Self-talk is that inner voice you use to converse with yourself. Listen to it and evaluate what it's telling you.

As is true for other exercises in this workbook, with self-talk you have to continue practicing and applying what you've learned. If you're in a domestic abuse group, talk about the effects of negative self-talk, but also share with the group when you've been successful at replacing negative messages with positive ones, or at least neutral ones. If you used positive self-talk and it resulted in changed thinking or behavior, document how that helped you. It's important that we note the progress we're making during this change process.

Jealousy

Simple fact: Men and women get jealous. Most of us have experienced jealousy. Yet for some men who batter, jealousy becomes a life-consuming emotion that distorts reality. A jealous man questions everything his partner does and feels: her trust, fidelity, love, and commitment. He gets jealous if she buys new clothes, puts on makeup, or gets a new hairstyle. He gets jealous if she talks on the phone, texts, writes letters, writes in a journal or diary, uses social networks, or goes out with friends. In our groups these men constantly blame their partners' unfaithfulness for their violence, even though their suspicions are often unjustified.

Feelings of jealousy, especially for men who batter, are tied to a belief that you have a claim to your partner: "She's *my* wife (or *my* girlfriend)." Some men are possessive from the beginning of a relationship. Many battered women have told me that their partners became extremely possessive right after the couple said "I do" or when they started living together. These men grew jealous or suspicious if the woman's behavior did not conform to the man's expectations, even if the couple hadn't yet had time to discuss what they expected from each other in the relationship.

Dave talked about two women he battered:

> It was almost a sadistic thing, like I was a military interrogator with a cigarette in his mouth. With her being only fifteen, I was able to manipulate her with questions. I would be in a good mood and ask her questions about men, and she would think it was okay to tell me about past relationships or men that she still found attractive. Then I would slap her. She would cry, not understanding what I was doing. I would hit her and apologize and then start the whole process over again. I must have slapped her at least two dozen times one night.
>
> I never trusted people, especially women. I always thought that women tried to get men to look at them or make a pass at them even if they were attached or married. I remember one time Lori was in this bowling league, and she wanted to get a new outfit. I went with her to the store and helped her pick out this really sexy top. She had such a beautiful body, and I told her how great she looked in it and that she should get it. Eight hours later I was saying, "You son of a bitch, I saw the way you were crossing your legs." Then I accused her of wearing provocative clothes even though I had picked the clothes out.

If you're a man who has battered, your jealousy could be based on the following:

Reactions to your violence: Deep down you know that your abusive and controlling behavior has had a profound impact on your current or former partner. The effects of your past actions could be driving your partner away or eroding the intimacy between you. Your relationship may already be over or is on shaky ground. Your jealousy (fear that she's leaving you) may be accurate because the relationship has been severely damaged.

False perceptions: If your partner and you are trying to work through your problems, you may still be uncertain about the future and have suspicions because the trust between the two of you has been strained. Since the violence started, you probably have become more possessive and controlling. Your relationship might be on life support, but now all of your partner's actions are under scrutiny.

Dave finally came to terms with his jealousy and possessiveness after he completed his domestic abuse group and went into treatment. He said the following:

> I knew I had to make a lot of changes. I needed to let go of my jealousy. In my relationship now, I accept that Kris has her own life and her own friends. I'm also more supportive of her and willing to listen to what she's saying, instead of just reacting.
>
> I remember in group this counselor said, "If nothing changes, then nothing will change." It sounded strange, but it made sense to me, because I needed to change.

Your jealousy may not be as intense as Dave's, but the kind of distrust he had in his relationships only breeds resentment. *Jealousy is a complicated emotion. Holding on to the negative feelings it triggers isn't helpful to you or your partner, so let's try to understand what's going on.*

EXERCISE 2

Handling Jealousy

> Before beginning make sure you're in a quiet place where you won't be interrupted. Take some deep breaths to relax and clear your mind.

Part 1: Please review the following example exercise.

1. Think of a time when you were very jealous with your current or past partner. This should be an incident when your *perceptions* about what was going on turned out to be false.

   We had been arguing a lot about one of our kids, Ben, who was in trouble. The fights were pretty bad, and we both said some things to each other that weren't very nice. She gave me the silent treatment and was late coming home from work. She didn't call, and I was consumed with jealousy.

2. What thoughts and feelings did you have?

   I felt suspicious, scared, angry, embarrassed, and insecure.

3. Did you create or "fan the flames" of your jealous feelings?

   I probably made things worse. I called and texted her about twenty times, each time leaving an angry message.

4. What actually occurred?

   Her cell phone was dead and she was stuck in traffic.

5. How could you handle these jealous feelings differently in the future?

   I need to make a commitment to myself to wait to resolve problems with Janelle when we're in a better place. I shouldn't have jumped to conclusions.

Part 2: Please answer the following questions.

1. Think of a time when you were very jealous with your current or past partner. This should be an incident when your *perceptions* about what was going on turned out to be false.

   _____

   _____

2. What thoughts and feelings did you have?

_____

_____

_____

3. Did you create or "fan the flames" of your jealous feelings?

_____

_____

_____

4. What actually occurred?

_____

_____

_____

5. How could you handle these jealous feelings differently in the future?

_____

_____

_____

> If you're in a domestic abuse group, discuss this exercise together, preferably in small groups. Each participant should talk about what he learned from the exercise.

A Closing Note

As you can see after completing this exercise, jealousy *can* be based in reality, but it is often a matter of perception. When there has been domestic abuse in a relationship, minor incidents or misunderstandings can get blown way out of proportion. If you're feeling jealous, you can make use of the self-talk skills you've practiced, discuss your emotions in your domestic abuse group, or talk to friends about what you're feeling.

Think about what you're learned so far. In earlier chapters we discussed the importance of being trusting and supportive of your partner. Hopefully you have come to the conclusion that your partner has a right to have her own friends and to spend time as she wishes—this doesn't have to make you feel jealous. And if someone finds your partner attractive, it does not have to be threatening. Trust is earned and develops over time; it cannot be imposed by making demands or controlling another person.

For some men the thought of losing their relationship is unbearable. They become desperate, and their jealousy becomes an obsession. A desperate man may think about his partner all the time. He may try to think about something else, yet images of her with another person slip into his mind, setting off feelings of anger and pain. He cannot imagine living without her. As I recommend in the book *Violent No More,* if you're feeling a sense of desperation, please see a counselor.

Letting Go

Letting go of a relationship is never easy. Some couples make a mutual decision that the relationship can't work. Although reaching that decision is painful and hard, at the end of the day there is some relief at being free from acrimony or a loveless relationship. If you were the one who made the decision to terminate the relationship, you may feel a sense of liberation. That relief can be short-lived, however, if you realize you acted impulsively and you now have regrets.

If your partner has decided to leave you and the decision is not mutual, your feelings of rejection may cause intense heartache and sorrow. Emotionally you might feel crushed. You may question your worth. You may be fixated on what you think you did wrong. You may wonder if you are flawed in some way. You may be preoccupied by the idea that she's leaving you for someone "better." You might dwell on thoughts that you'll never have someone in your life again.

Men and women experience similar feelings when they are rejected. But men and women typically (although not always) process their feelings differently. Women reach out to their friends and families. They deal with issues, analyze what happened, and give and receive support. For women, expressing feelings is embraced and encouraged. But most of us men have an extremely hard time talking about our feelings. We may experience gut-wrenching emotional pain, but we're taught to "suck it up" or "be a man." When a relationship ends, we men don't typically call our friends and talk for hours about the sadness we feel. We usually don't cry. We usually don't have a support system, ask for help, or seek counseling. We face our grief like we think we're supposed to: alone.

If you do have a support system, your friends may give you the kind of advice that really isn't helpful. "She wasn't worth it." "You're better off without her." They may think they're being supportive, but their assessment of what happened may just fuel your newfound contempt for the very person you once loved.

Men who batter often abuse alcohol or drugs when their partners end a relationship. When they're intoxicated, their emotions may ooze out, allowing them to temporarily talk about their sadness. Or the resentment and bitterness might only grow stronger. It doesn't have to be this way.

For men who have battered an intimate partner, rejection and the termination of a relationship take on added significance. You know at some core level that your violence and abuse precipitated her decision to leave. The pain of rejection often turns to anger or cynicism.

Concentrate on how you can let go of your relationship, experience the grief, learn from your mistakes, and get on with your life. If you're in a new relationship, or hope to be in one in the future, you have newfound knowledge about what a respectful intimate relationship can be like and new skills to help you create one. In the future, refuse to be possessive and jealous.

Commit to being trusting and supportive of your partner. Discard beliefs that allow you to feel entitled to call the shots in the relationship. Pledge to not being abusive when you're having conflicts.

If you're hurting because of the loss of your relationship, know that the pain is part of a natural healing process and that the painful feelings will eventually pass. You may need some help with these new commitments. You may need some help from a counselor. *The following exercise can give you some perspective.*

> Before beginning make sure you're in a quiet place where you won't be interrupted. Take some deep breaths to relax and clear your mind.

Part 1: Please review the following example exercise.

1. If your relationship has ended, or you think it could end in the near future, you might be upset, angry, or sad. Yet most men also experience some loss and grief over what they will miss about the relationship. List examples of what you will miss.

   - *having dinner together and intimate times*
   - *celebrating special occasions*
   - *taking trips*
   - *socializing: going out with friends and being with family*
   - *talking about our day*
   - *going to events with the kids*
   - *working on home projects together*

2. For each example above try to think of a way you can continue to get your emotional needs met even though your relationship is over. Think of ways you can bolster your spirits. When you feel lonely or depressed, look back at this list—it can be healing. Are there other things you can do?

   - *spend more time with friends and family*
   - *explore new interests*
   - *spend quality time with the children, even though I'm not with my partner*
   - *get involved with community organizations*
   - *develop new friendships*
   - *play sports that I enjoy*
   - *read more*
   - *go to counseling*
   - *acknowledge that being sad is okay and that it will pass*

3. If you are experiencing negative or hurtful feelings about your partner or ex-partner, think about the steps you can take to avoid harassing or being hurtful toward her, and consider ways you can bolster your spirits during this difficult time.

   - *stay in my counseling group longer*
   - *use positive self-talk and try not to dwell on the loss*
   - *avoid saying negative things about her in front of the children*
   - *respect her decision if she doesn't want contact with me*
   - *not violate the protection order*
   - *work on not blaming her or myself*
   - *see a counselor to help me sort out these issues*

Part 2: Please answer the following questions.

1. If your relationship has ended, or you think it could end in the near future, you might be upset, angry, or sad. Yet most men also experience some loss and grief over what they will miss about the relationship. List examples of what you will miss.

   _____

   _____

   _____

   _____

   _____

   _____

2. For each example above, try to think of a way you can continue to get your emotional needs met even though your relationship is over. Think of ways you can bolster your spirits. When you feel lonely or depressed look back at this list—it can be healing. Are there other things you can do?

   _____

   _____

   _____

   _____

   _____

   _____

3. If you are having negative or hurtful feelings about your partner or ex-partner, think about the steps you can take to avoid harassing or being hurtful toward her, and consider ways you can bolster your spirits during this difficult time.

_____

_____

_____

_____

_____

_____

> If you're in a domestic abuse group, discuss this exercise together, preferably in small groups. Each participant should talk about what he learned from the exercise.

A Closing Thought

Not all men will experience loss when their relationship ends. Some men will welcome the cessation of the relationship, even though they are responsible for the violence. For some men, and certainly for the partners they abused, there simply has been too much animosity and pain, and too many bad feelings. Sadly since some of these men won't take the time to understand how their violence affected their relationships, they will get into "rebound" relationships, and the abusive patterns will start all over again.

If you are truly saddened by the loss of your relationship, however, hopefully this exercise allowed you to examine what you might miss and what you need to do to get your needs met so you're not isolated and not constantly dwelling on your loss. When my mother died, a friend of mine whom I hadn't talked to for years left me a voicemail message saying that he had lost his mom, too. He said, "Though it might seem hard now, you'll get through it, and you won't be thinking of her so much." At the time, I thought it was a rather insensitive message. But he was right. I still think about my mother a lot, but I'm not immobilized by the loss. Like most people I have had my share of intimate relationships that have ended and loved ones who have passed away. We do get through it.

Let go of bitter feelings that you may still harbor about your partner or ex-partner, and reject any thoughts of getting back at her because you feel betrayed. Although you may feel hurt and angry now, revenge is senseless, can be dangerous, and in the end harms you. Refrain from blaming her. She may have made mistakes in the relationship, but if she wants to move on, you need to honor her decision. Grieving is natural, and there is no set time limit for when it will end.

Making Changes and Staying on Track

In this chapter you will explore some of the challenges of staying together after the abuse has ended. Topics addressed include: (1) understanding and accepting your partner's anger, a critical step if you want to stay in a relationship with the partner whom you abused; (2) changing your mind-set regarding the sexist and stereotypical messages that get in the way of your becoming a man who supports equality in relationships; (3) getting your needs met without being abusive; and (4) taking time-outs when you think you may become violent or abusive.

Understanding and Accepting Your Partner's Anger

Men and women get angry. Anger is a very natural emotional response when our boundaries are violated, when we are threatened with bodily harm, or when an injustice occurs against us or others. When stress, tension, or bad moods consume us we might get angry and lash out over little things. Some days we get angry at our children or our partners, react in a negative manner at work, or get aggravated while driving on the freeway. Rather than responding to problems with a positive and peaceful mind, we let anger overwhelm us, and we say or do inappropriate things. We usually regret those outbursts.

> *You are never strong enough that you don't need help.*
> — CESAR CHAVEZ

For men who batter, anger can be a strategic tactic to intimidate their partner or shut down discussion. Men who batter use their anger as a warning sign that violence is right around the corner. As discussed earlier, men who batter know that intimidation—angry looks, pounding on tables, slamming doors, throwing things, screaming—brings immediate results.

Women also get angry in intimate relationships; they glare, slam doors, throw and break things, and yell and scream. The difference is that the power imbalance between men and women usually means that a woman's anger is unlikely to intimidate her partner or shut him down, unless he's afraid of her. If you are afraid of your partner, I urge you to seek help. When I was the men's program coordinator at the Domestic Abuse Intervention Project, I assisted men in getting civil orders for protection and helped them figure out how they could safely get out of their relationships. Although I offered this help, few men requested it; they were usually able to leave a relationship with an abusive partner on their own because they didn't fear physical retaliation or being stalked.

Men in general don't like it when their partners get angry. A man who batters frequently minimizes, trivializes, challenges, threatens, or uses violence to block his partner's anger. *Has this been your experience? Let's take a look at this issue.*

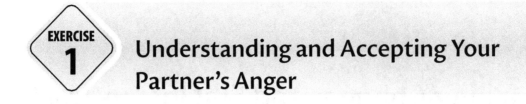

EXERCISE 1 — Understanding and Accepting Your Partner's Anger

The following exercise is designed to help you understand what motivated you when you tried to block your partner's anger by minimizing, trivializing, challenging, threatening, or using violence as a reaction.

> Before beginning make sure you're in a quiet place where you won't be interrupted. Take some deep breaths to relax and clear your mind.

Part 1: Please review the following examples of blocking your partner's anger.

Minimizing your partner's anger involves trying to convince her that she's overreacting.

Examples of minimizing

- "Why do you get hysterical over such little things?"
- "Why are you making such a big deal out of this?"
- "I don't know what you're talking about."
- "You have no reason to be angry about that."
- "You don't see me getting bent out of shape when you _____, do you?"

Trivializing your partner's anger involves being sarcastic or using put-downs.

Examples of trivializing

- "Yeah, you're right, you're always right, so you can stop being angry."
- "I do one little thing, and now look at you."
- "It must be that time of the month."
- "If you would just grow up, you wouldn't be reacting this way."
- "You sound just like your mother!"
- "You're cute when you're angry."

Challenging your partner's anger involves cutting her off or questioning her anger. You might compare something *she* did in the past to the issue she's angry at you about, refuse to talk things through, or turn the tables on her.

Examples of challenging

- "What about when you _____?"
- "As if you've never _____ before."
- "Well, if that's the way you feel, I'm out of here."
- "I'm not listening to this shit anymore."
- "You don't care about my feelings."
- "Maybe you should go see a shrink to deal with these problems you have."
- "If you didn't hang around with _____, you wouldn't be acting like this."

Threatening or using violence is an extreme way to block your partner's anger.

Examples of threatening or using violence

- saying "Shut up, or else!"
- screaming back at her or yelling loudly in her face
- using threatening gestures or throwing something at her or at the wall
- hitting her
- holding her by the arms or putting your hand over her mouth

Part 2: Please review the following example exercise.

1. Describe an incident when you tried to block your partner's anger.

   Tyra got angry at me when I asked her where she'd been. I thought it was a harmless question, and we got into an argument.

2. Describe your feelings at the time.

   Defensive. Misunderstood. Angry. Picked on. Hurt.

3. Describe your thoughts at the time.

   She's saying these things purposely to make me angry. I don't deserve this. She's overreacting. I'm not going to take this anymore. She'd better stop, or I'm leaving.

4. How did you respond to her anger?

   I yelled at her and called her a fuckin' bitch.

5. How could you have handled the situation differently?

   I could have chosen not to respond when she got angry. I guess I could have discussed her reaction with her at a later date and acknowledged to myself that she may have thought I was checking up on her. I need to remember what I'm learning in group about why she continues to be angry with me even though I stopped using violence.

Part 3: Please review the following example exercise.

In this case the man's partner was angry with him, but he responded to her anger appropriately.

1. What was the issue that your partner was angry about?

   I didn't give Jeanne the message that her sister called. I told her I forgot, and I apologized. She said this kind of thing happens a lot. We started to argue.

2. Describe your feelings at the time.

   Attacked. Angry. Defensive.

3. Describe your thoughts at the time.

   I thought she was blowing things out of proportion, but I also thought that maybe what she was saying might be true.

4. How did you respond to her anger?

   I listened to her rather than arguing. I used positive self-talk and tried to understand why she was upset. I was assertive but not aggressive. I didn't turn her anger around so that I would become angry and blame her.

5. How did you feel after handling a tense situation in a positive manner?

   It felt good to have a disagreement that was settled without our usual yelling and accusing.

Part 4: Please answer the following questions.

1. Describe a time when you minimized your partner's anger by trying to convince her that she was overreacting.

   _____

   _____

   _____

   _____

2. Describe a time when you trivialized your partner's anger by being sarcastic or using put-downs.

   _____

   _____

   _____

3. Describe a time when you challenged your partner's anger by cutting her off or questioning her anger.

_____

_____

_____

_____

4. Describe a time when you used or threatened to use violence to block your partner's anger.

_____

_____

_____

_____

Part 5: Describe a recent incident when your partner was angry with you and you responded to her anger appropriately.

1. What was the issue that your partner was angry about?

_____

_____

_____

_____

2. Describe your feelings at the time.

_____

_____

_____

3. Describe your thoughts at the time.

_____

_____

_____

_____

4. How did you respond to her anger?

_____

_____

_____

_____

5. How did you feel after handling a tense situation in a positive manner?

_____

_____

_____

_____

> **If you're in a domestic abuse group, discuss this exercise together, preferably in small groups. Each participant should talk about what he learned from the exercise.**

A Closing Thought

Hopefully this exercise helped you to understand what was motivating you when you tried to block your partner's anger by minimizing, trivializing, challenging, or convincing your partner that she was overreacting. When you've tried to block your partner's anger, her response was probably outrage, disgust, and more anger. Compare that response with an example when you didn't get defensive and responded to her anger appropriately. Responding appropriately (without getting defensive or angry in return) might have taken some effort on your part, because it wasn't your usual response. Hopefully the results were more mutually satisfactory and you recognized your reaction as progress.

If you are going to stay together, you need to understand that your partner most likely has significant anger—and it's probably right below the surface. Whether your violence was constant or infrequent, the memories of being abused and humiliated may be unforgettable. Little things, conversations, and anniversaries may remind her of an argument or a beating.

As M'Liss, whose story appears in *Violent No More*, said:

> *Chuck had beaten me up when we were traveling in northern Minnesota because I'd left a blanket where we'd camped. It was the kind of thing Chuck would get angry about. Well, years later, when Chuck had stopped abusing me, we decided to take a car trip to Canada. When we drove by the park where he had beaten me, I asked him if he remembered beating me there, because it brought back painful memories for me. He got really defensive and asked why I was always bringing up the past. It's strange because I don't bring up the past that much, but he thinks I do.*

If you're committed to repairing the relationship with the intimate partner whom you abused, you must stay focused on your commitments. You've made promises to her and to yourself. It is understandable that her trust level with you is probably fairly low. If you have attended your domestic abuse groups and are practicing the exercises in this workbook, a more enlightened man has emerged. You now understand that there will always be disagreements, but you hopefully are gaining a more heightened awareness of your actions and reactions. You honor your pledge to remain nonviolent.

Changing Your Mind-Set

Change is a process. We can't just will a transformation in our thinking to occur. We've had years of being subjected to a culture that teaches boys and men to be a certain way, and now we're wisely questioning those societal messages. It's good that we're questioning, because the status quo has certainly not benefited women and girls. In the United States, we have very high rates of domestic violence, rape, and sex trafficking. Nor has the status quo been good for men and boys. Large numbers of men are incarcerated in our prisons for acts of violence, boys and young men needlessly die from gang violence, and men have a suicide rate that is three to four times higher than that of females.

Another reason for changing our mind-set is to improve our chances of having healthy intimate relationships. Men who have made significant changes in their thinking and have altered their behavior first took the initiative to gain a deeper understanding of their beliefs and attitudes about men, women, and relationships. They were open to being challenged about their sense of male entitlement (having expectations or privileges because of their gender). They read books that provided insight. They volunteered to enter counseling, or if they were court-ordered to attend a domestic abuse group, they eventually opened up and participated in the process.

Maybe you're ready to dig deeper. Maybe you're open to exploring new ideas. You might feel a little uncomfortable at first. Men don't want to admit they are sexist—I know I don't. In many ways it's similar to white people not wanting to be perceived as racist. As a white person in this society I recognize that I have privilege and that I walk through the world very differently than does a person of color. Similarly, as a man, wherever I am on this earth I have privileges and benefits that women don't, even though I strive not to be sexist.

In the following exercise we'll examine the sexist and stereotypical messages that males have been exposed to. *Have these messages had an impact on you as an adult? Have they had an effect on your intimate relationships?*

EXERCISE
2

Changing Your Mind-Set

> Before beginning make sure you're in a quiet place where you won't be interrupted. Take some deep breaths to relax and clear your mind.

Part 1: Please review the following examples of changing one's mind-set.

1. Make a list of all the stereotypical and sexist messages you've heard as a boy and as an adult about men, women, and relationships.

   - *Men must be tough. Women are weak.*
   - *Women are too emotional.*
   - *The man is the head of the household.*
   - *It's okay for men to get angry. Men settle disagreements through violence.*
   - *Women provoke men to use violence.*
   - *Men have uncontrollable sexual urges.*
   - *If a woman dresses provocatively, she's asking for it.*
   - *Men are the breadwinners.*
   - *Women take care of the house and children.*

2. What has been the impact of these beliefs on your life?

   - *Because of my attitudes, women don't trust me.*
   - *I don't show my emotions or talk about my feelings.*
   - *I feel inadequate because I don't make enough money.*
   - *I haven't had a long term-relationship.*
   - *I have assaulted my last two partners.*
   - *I get into a lot of bar fights for stupid reasons.*

3. How have these beliefs affected your relationship with your current partner or ex-partner?

   - *My expectations of men and women have led to arguments.*
   - *My girlfriend got an order for protection against me.*
   - *I don't talk with my partner about my feelings and what's going on in my life.*
   - *I feel inadequate as a husband and father.*
   - *I've never trusted women since I was dumped.*

4. How has your thinking about these kinds of gender stereotypes changed?

- *I'm more aware of how my son is being influenced by sexism.*
- *From my domestic abuse groups, I see that these stereotypical beliefs are shared by a lot of men.*
- *I'm trying to talk about my feelings with my wife.*
- *I see now that I don't get to have everything my way.*

Part 2: Please answer the following questions.

1. Make a list of all the stereotypical and sexist messages you've heard as a boy and as an adult about men, women, and relationships.

_____

_____

_____

2. What has been the impact of these beliefs on your life?

_____

_____

_____

3. How have these beliefs affected your relationship with your current partner or ex-partner?

_____

_____

_____

4. How has your thinking about these kinds of gender stereotypes changed?

_____

_____

_____

> If you're in a domestic abuse group, discuss this exercise together, preferably in small groups. Each participant should talk about what he learned from the exercise.

A Closing Thought

In our domestic abuse groups we sometimes talk about the mindset we hold about masculinity. When men feel comfortable being a little vulnerable, we can discuss the price we all pay for conforming to rigid expectations about what being a "real man" means. We can talk about how we're constantly being pressured to prove ourselves. Men worry that if they don't "match up" or are perceived as weak they will be ridiculed or judged harshly by women and other men. Men are taught not to back down in the face of a confrontation and not to express emotions except anger and cynicism.

When men get stuck in this kind of thinking, they become inflexible and unfeeling. Society tends to define masculinity as men having strength and courage. There's nothing wrong with these attributes as long as we're also committed to having the strength and courage to be men who care, who love our families, and who are nonviolent.

After completing this exercise, hopefully you've recognized how your current mind-set has gotten in the way of your having a supportive and respectful intimate relationship. Your mind-set has very likely contributed to your violence, but you *can* change it.

Getting Your Needs Met Without Being Abusive

As I discussed in the book *Violent No More,* boys are taught to be aggressive. To survive on the playground, in the neighborhood, or within an abusive family, boys are constantly being tested. They tease and taunt, give and receive insults, shove and hit each other, sometimes landing the blows and sometimes enduring them. This is a boy's world. To get their needs met, or to be accepted, many boys quickly learn to be aggressive.

In professional sports it seems perfectly acceptable for one player to get mad at—and sometimes physically attack—another. The public accepts this behavior, cheering as both benches clear in a baseball game and the players duke it out. Professional wrestlers feign anger to inspire the roars of admiring fans eager for someone to get stomped or have a folding chair slammed over his head. A hockey player may drop his gloves and attempt to land as many blows as possible on an opponent's head before the referees finally stop the fight. I recently watched a video of a pee-wee hockey game during which nine- and ten-year-old boys got into a confrontation on the ice, clearly mimicking the brawling they saw taking place at professional hockey games.

Aggression is part of the male world of anger, violence, and power. Sadly it is expected and accepted. Most boys adjust and survive childhood and adolescence, even though we all lose a bit of our innocence and some of our ability to be vulnerable and sensitive. And as most men know, our families aren't exempt from the violence.

As Hector said in the book *Violent No More:*

> *My home life had an incredible influence on the decisions I made as a young man. At seventeen I was very altruistic about my purpose in life. I always wanted to join the military and serve my country. Of course there were two other big reasons for wanting to enlist. First, I wanted to get out of the house as fast as I could. And second, I knew in the military that I could fight, and I wanted to fight. This may*

seem counterintuitive, but I guess being around all of that violence had an impact on me. My instinct was to survive—whether from my father's fists or from living in the 'hood.

A man who batters often perceives arguments and conflicts with his partner as a test of wills, like the childhood and adolescent tests of "manning up." In our groups men frequently claim that in order to get their needs met they must be aggressive and prevent their partners from getting the upper hand. Being disrespected by a woman is not to be tolerated. During an argument they might storm out of the house, swear, refuse to talk, decline attempts to negotiate, threaten their partner, or become violent. *Does this sound familiar? Can you get your needs met without being controlling and abusive? Can you work through your problems in a respectful manner? Let's see how this can work.*

Being Assertive, Not Aggressive

Two key elements for being assertive are: (1) having the willingness to ask for what you need without being demanding, controlling, or threatening and (2) being able to express your feelings without attacking or shaming.

> Before beginning make sure you're in a quiet place where you won't be interrupted. Take some deep breaths to relax and clear your mind.

Part 1: Please review the following example exercise.

1. Describe an incident when you were aggressive with your current or former partner.

   I was angry because I told Alicia that I need her to be home to watch the kids so I could get to my softball game. I had the kids, and she left anyway.

2. List the aggressive words you used.

   I think I said, "Goddamnit, Alicia, now I'm late for my game. Next Friday you'll have to get a babysitter, because I'm out of here at five." I probably said some other choice words.

3. Describe the tone of your voice.

   Not screaming, but yelling.

4. Describe your body language, especially anything that might be considered intimidating behavior.

   Ran toward the car when she pulled up, showing her my anger.

5. Remember the feelings you had during the incident. From what you now know about being assertive rather than aggressive, how could you have expressed your feelings or opinions without being controlling or abusive (aggressive)?

   I knew as soon as I started to run to the car that she would get scared. I didn't need to do that. I could have waited until she got in the house or talked with her later. I didn't even give her a chance to explain—I just went off on her. I guess being assertive rather than aggressive would mean trying to ensure that in the future we both can meet our obligations. I need to be clearer (without being threatening) that my Friday game is important to me.

Part 2: Please answer the following questions.

1. Describe a recent example when you were aggressive with your current or former partner.

_____

_____

_____

2. List the aggressive words you used.

_____

_____

3. Describe the tone of your voice.

_____

_____

4. Describe your body language, especially anything that might be considered intimidating behavior.

_____

_____

5. Remember the feelings you had during the incident. From what you now know about being assertive rather than aggressive, how could you have expressed your feelings or opinions without being controlling or abusive (aggressive)?

_____

_____

_____

_____

> If you're in a domestic abuse group, discuss this exercise together, preferably in small groups. Each participant should talk about what he learned from the exercise.

A Closing Thought

Disagreements are inevitable in an intimate relationship. This exercise demonstrates that there is a clear distinction between being aggressive and being assertive. When men who batter are aggressive they use angry gestures, intimidating words, a bullying tone of voice, and threatening body language to get their way. Since disagreements are inescapable, you have to make the choice whether you'll be assertive or aggressive. You *can* express your feelings and communicate your needs or opinions in a manner that doesn't disregard or disrespect your partner.

If your goal is simply to get what you want, being assertive can still be controlling even if you're not being intimidating. If your goal is to always be right, to always get your way, and to always win, it's hard to have a respectful relationship. Couples need to develop patterns of communicating, negotiating, and compromising that resolve problems in a mutually satisfying manner. The next chapter explores these methods and offers some useful guidelines.

Taking Time-Outs

As explained in the book *Violent No More,* taking a time-out means removing yourself from a potentially explosive situation without becoming violent. This practice may seem simplistic, but it works. However, it only works as long as you're not taking a time-out to avoid conflict or using a time-out as a means to further control your partner. For time-outs to be effective, you should be working at the same time on changing the beliefs that many men who batter hold about women and about their role as men in intimate relationships. Here's how it works.

What to Do and Where to Go

Take a time-out anytime you feel you may become abusive. Make a commitment to removing yourself from a situation that might otherwise result in your intimidating, threatening, emotionally abusing, or hitting your partner.

When people get angry, it's usually because they aren't getting what they want or because someone is doing something they don't like. Taking a time-out does not address the causes of your anger, but it does provide an instant tool to help you avoid situations in which you might become abusive.

When you get angry or agitated, you usually have emotional or physical feelings. On an emotional level, you may feel hurt, defensive, or mad. Your mind becomes engulfed with anger, and you feel an urge to vent your feelings. On a physical level, you may feel your fists or teeth clenching together, tightness in your stomach or neck, tension in the body, or a headache.

These emotional and physical feelings are cues that angry responses and possibly violence are on the way. Pay attention to these signs. When you feel that you cannot express yourself in a nonabusive or nonviolent manner, take a time-out and leave.

You can use a time-out to get away from a potentially abusive situation, such as an argument between your partner and you that is about to begin or that has escalated. Perhaps you have been thinking about present problems or past issues and feel yourself growing angry. Recognize the emotional and physical changes in yourself, listen to what your body is telling you, and get ready to take a time-out.

Here Are the Steps

First, calmly tell your partner that you are taking a time-out. You may prefer to write a note or send a text. You might say, "I'm feeling upset and angry, and I need to take a time-out." By stating this clearly you let your partner know you are taking responsibility for your actions and leaving to avoid becoming abusive.

Second, let your partner know how long the time-out will last. You might say, "I'm feeling upset and angry and I need a time-out. I'll be back in one hour." Never stay away longer than you have indicated without calling or texting to let your partner know. This is so your partner will not be left wondering when you might return or be scared or startled when you do.

During your time-out, do not use alcohol or drugs. Do not drive. Take a walk; that's often the best way to relax. You may want to talk with a friend or someone from your domestic abuse group if you are in one. Whatever the conflict, use the time-out to think positively about yourself, your partner, and the relationship. Remind yourself that you are a good person, that your partner is a good person, and that separately or together the two of you will be able to resolve the conflict in due time.

Many conflicts between partners arise over unresolved issues that come out in different ways. Silence, bad moods, and leaving often mask what is really going on. Letting unresolved issues fester is not helpful to your relationship and keeps your partner on pins and needles. Talk about these issues with a counselor. Even if the issue isn't resolved, take a time-out if you think you're going to be abusive.

Although I recommend taking time-outs to the men in my groups, I am also aware that some men use them to avoid working on problems. If you take a time-out every time you have a disagreement, your actions will be not only controlling but also self-defeating. Use time-outs with a constructive purpose in mind. Please review the following time-out rules.

Time-Out Rules

1. Take a time-out when you recognize your cues and before you become emotionally or physically abusive.

2. Take a time-out when you feel like you're going to become abusive or violent; do not take a time-out to avoid conflict.

3. Tell your partner you are taking a time-out.

4. Tell your partner how long you'll be gone.

5. Do not drink, use drugs, or drive.

6. Call or text a friend or group member for support.

7. Do calming exercises like walking, shooting free throws at a basketball court, or meditating.

8. Think positive thoughts. Do not dwell on the problem that caused you to become angry.

9. If you are still agitated, or if you believe that you might still become abusive or violent if you go home, and you need more time than you agreed to, call or text your partner and let her know.

10. Your partner is not obliged to take a time-out; you take a time-out for yourself.

11. If your partner indicates that she is afraid of you, stay away. Find an alternative place to stay until things have calmed down.

12. When you return, do not insist that your partner and you resolve the conflict you were having.

13. If you notice your cues again, take another time-out.

14. Whenever you follow the time-out rules, make a note of the positive way you handled the situation and its results.

> If you are going to use time-outs in your relationship, review this section and the previous one with your partner. Go through the time-out rules when you're both in a calm mood. Practice a time-out when you are not angry so that your partner and you understand the process and each other's expectations. Your partner needs to know the rules of the time-out so she knows what to expect. *Your partner is under no obligation to help you with this exercise.*

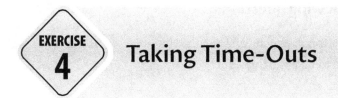

EXERCISE 4

Taking Time-Outs

Now you know the expectations and conditions of taking a time-out. If you are in a domestic abuse program or in counseling and you have reviewed the time-out rules, you may be ready (if you're in an intimate relationship) to put time-outs into practice. If you have used a time-out in the last thirty days, complete the following exercise.

> Before beginning make sure you're in a quiet place where you won't be interrupted. Take some deep breaths to relax and clear your mind.

Part 1: Please answer the following questions.

1. Describe how you explained the process of taking a time-out to your partner prior to actually taking one.

_____

_____

_____

_____

2. What were your partner's perceptions of your desire to try taking a time-out? How did she feel about it?

_____

_____

_____

3. After discussing the process with you, was she open to the concept? If not, did you honor her request?

_____

_____

Assuming she was open to your taking the time-out, complete Part 2 of the exercise.

Part 2: Please answer the following questions.

1. Describe in some detail the situation in which you took the time-out. What were the setting and the issue that led you to take the time-out?

_____

_____

_____

_____

_____

_____

2. What were you feeling emotionally? Physically?

_____

_____

3. What were you thinking?

_____

_____

4. How did you explain to your partner that you wanted to take a time-out?

_____

_____

5. How did you leave? Where did you go? What did you do during the time-out?

_____

_____

6. Did you calm down? What kinds of self-talk did you use?

_____

_____

_____

7. Did you communicate with your partner while you were gone? If so, what did you say, and what was her response?

_____

_____

8. When you returned, how did you communicate with your partner about the issue that got you to the point where you felt you needed to take a time-out? Did you take responsibility for your part in the disagreement?

_____

_____

> If you're in a domestic abuse group, discuss this exercise together, preferably in small groups. Each participant should talk about what he learned from the exercise.

A Closing Thought

The time-out is probably a new exercise for you. Like any new practice you'll need to be consistent and make changes if it isn't working. For instance, if your partner tells you that she felt frightened when you left, you probably didn't leave soon enough, and you may not have communicated your reason for leaving in a manner that she considered clear and nonthreatening. Talk about your time-outs in your domestic abuse group or with a counselor.

If you're in a new intimate relationship, I hope you'll consider telling your partner about your past. You don't need to reveal every little detail, but your partner deserves to know that you had a domestic abuse problem. Tell your partner how you worked through your problems and some of the tools that you've used and continue to use to stay violence free, including taking time-outs. Completing your domestic abuse program and the exercises in the workbook doesn't mean that old responses to conflicts won't resurface in the future. As Chuck, a group participant, said:

> I'd be a liar if I said I haven't come close to being violent on occasion. A couple can learn to put the brakes on things when they escalate. For me it's like driving down the freeway at sixty miles an hour and putting on the emergency brake—the wheels lock up, the brakes are smoking, and you come to a quick and complete stop.

As Elliot said:

> I try to apply some of the tools I learned in the program. I take time-outs and try to use self-talk when I feel myself going back to old patterns.

A Note to Counselors

As I pointed out in the book *Violent No More,* there is an ongoing debate among practitioners who run domestic abuse groups over the efficacy of teaching skill-building practices to men who haven't changed their beliefs about women, men, and entitlement. Some programs have stopped teaching anger management techniques like time-outs altogether.

The concern raised by some in the field is that men who continue to devalue women and don't want to give up their dominant role in an intimate relationship will simply misuse skill-based techniques to further control their partners.

I share these concerns, especially with regard to men who don't want to change. Yet for men who *do* want to change, time-outs, like other techniques in this workbook, work. In one program I was involved in, many partners of the men in my groups reported in surveys that the time-out was useful and provided a safety valve when there were disagreements and conflicts. The women felt safer because of the time-outs.

Like anything we teach in our groups, we can't control how it gets used or misused. Throughout this section I have tried to insert my cautions to men and women about the practice of taking time-outs.

Resolving Conflicts, Strengthening Relationships

When two people decide to move in together or get married, they usually experience some growing pains. When you're dating you share your thoughts about what your new merger might look like. It all seems very exciting. At this early stage potential problems don't seem like obstacles. Once you're sharing the same living space, however, you might find yourself dealing with issues you didn't anticipate. You may not have discussed some fundamental topics about living together.

Compatibility issues can be resolved over time if you work together in a cooperative manner, but many couples struggle. Differences over household responsibilities, money, child care, and the realities of sharing a home usually don't surface until you've moved in together. These differences can be even more difficult for men who have battered (because they are usually controlling) or who have fairly inflexible beliefs about the roles of men and women. Unless your partner shares your beliefs about gender roles, resentments can complicate the transition from single life to a partnership.

> *Darkness cannot drive out darkness—only light can do that. Hate cannot drive out hate—only love can do that.*
> — MARTIN LUTHER KING JR.

Traditional and Egalitarian Relationships

Some couples have what we might call a "traditional" relationship, in which the roles of men and women are fairly strictly defined. Women in traditional relationships do most of the cooking, house cleaning, and child care, even if the man and woman both have jobs. Men may share in some of those responsibilities, but usually to a lesser extent. Taking care of the car, shoveling snow, mowing the yard, fixing things, or taking out the garbage is typically the male domain. I grew up in a family that was clearly traditional. Even when my mother started working outside the home, she did most of the household work and took on most of the child-care responsibilities.

I advocate an egalitarian (equal) relationship not just because it has worked for me but also because it is consistent with the goals of being in an intimate partnership. In egalitarian relationships couples don't necessarily follow traditional gender roles, and they share in the household responsibilities. In addition to being a fairer system, egalitarian relationships permit men to go beyond feeling *obliged* to share in child care; rather, they desire the responsibilities of shared parenting and the rewards of being involved fathers. In egalitarian relationships men encourage and support partners who are pursuing new careers and community involvement. Men in egalitarian relationships are less likely to feel threatened by their partners' aspirations because they see their partners' growth as an enhancement of their relationship.

If you choose an egalitarian relationship, you may stumble a bit down this unfamiliar path and experience some confusion. That's okay. We all have the abilities to make an equal partnership work; we just need to apply them. Examine the Equality Wheel below. It's an illustration of what an egalitarian relationship looks like. As you can see there are many elements to an equal relationship. Review the Equality Wheel from time to time. Are you relating to your partner in a manner illustrated by the wheel? If not, review the guides on negotiating and fair discussion later in the chapter, and complete the exercises. They address topics such as sharing the load, handling money problems, learning to negotiate and compromise, and having fair discussions.

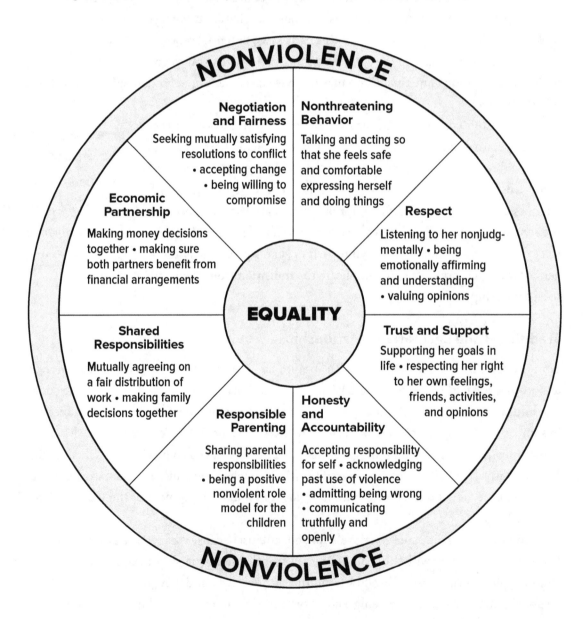

Sharing the Load

Sharing the load means finding an equitable division of labor to make your household work. If you believe that women should be subservient to men, sharing the load isn't likely to happen. If you believe in rigid gender roles and that women should be submissive, you probably expect your wife or girlfriend to cook all the meals, clean up after meals, maintain the house, and do the majority of child care. Your wife or girlfriend may be differential to your expectations because she's resigned to this role, she believes this is her status as a woman, or she's afraid of challenging your authority. She may have attempted to resist your domination in the past, but the resistance was met with punishment. Women in this situation either leave the relationship when they can or learn to adapt.

As Jim said in the book *Violent No More:*

> *One time I came home really drunk and demanded she make me a steak. I went into the kitchen and there were all these dirty dishes in the sink, and I flew into a rage. I started throwing the dishes at her and then I hit her in the face with the back of my hand. I started breaking everything in the house.*

As Emma said:

> *Throughout our marriage [John] had total control over me. He decided what music we would listen to, what television program we'd watch, what clothes I wore, and where and when we'd go out. At the time I wanted to be the woman who would stick by him no matter what, who would not leave him, and I was. He had told me all of the bad experiences he'd had with women in the past, and I really believed I could be a different kind of woman for him.*

When men who batter examine their failed relationships and recognize how their unyielding beliefs about gender roles have become obstacles to a healthy relationship, they may be open to change. *If you're willing to explore an egalitarian relationship, completing the following exercises can be an important first step.*

EXERCISE 1 — Cooperating with Your Partner

To help you understand how to share responsibilities in your relationship, complete the following exercise with your partner, if she is willing. If your relationship has ended, review the exercise anyway and try to recall whether you struggled with sharing the load with your ex-partner. Did you have unrealistic expectations of household responsibilities that in retrospect seem unfair? Was it difficult for you to compromise? How would you handle these kinds of issues in the future?

> As with all of the exercises in this workbook, your partner is under no obligation to participate in this one. You should not pressure her. Your past violence and abuse may be too hurtful, and her trust level with you may be compromised. Give her all of the time she needs to heal. If she's at the point where she *does* want to work on these elements of your relationship, you may proceed with her.

Please answer the following questions.

1. With your partner, make a list of your joint and separate responsibilities and obligations.
   Examples (add to the list as needed)
   - *pay the bills*
   - *cook the meals*
   - *wash the dishes*
   - *buy groceries*
   - *buy the children's clothes*
   - *read to the children/help with homework*
   - *take the children to the doctor, dentist, or extracurricular activities*
   - *do the yard work*
   - *clean the apartment or house*
   - *repair things in the home or arrange to have repairs done*
   - *wash and put away the laundry*
   - *take care of the car*
   - *arrange social contacts*
   - *pick children up from school or the bus stop*

* *take care of the pets*
* (list others)

_____

_____

_____

2. Next to each task, write the initials of the partner who always or usually does it.

3. Is your partner given more than her fair share of responsibilities?

_____

_____

_____

4. Can you compromise on an equitable distribution of the workload? If so, list the tasks and responsibilities that you'll work on. (Write your agreed-upon plan down in this workbook or in a notebook so you can assess your progress.)

_____

_____

_____

_____

_____

> If you're in a domestic abuse group, discuss this exercise together, preferably in small groups. Each participant should talk about what he learned from the exercise.

A Closing Thought

From time to time review the above exercise. Is the new plan that you agreed to working, or do you need to make modifications? Couples who don't communicate are destined for problems. For instance after completing this exercise you may have agreed that you would help the children with their homework more than you had done in the past. Check in with your partner about how you're doing. You might even set specific times of the month when you will discuss your plan and your progress. How did this increased involvement with your children feel for you? How does your partner feel about it? (Ask yourself similar questions about the other parts of your plan.) If you don't discuss what is going on, resentment can build. As each partner takes on new responsibilities, do either of you feel judged by the other? If the changes in the new division of labor are working, acknowledge your accomplishments.

Don't have these discussions or attempt to make these decisions when you're angry. This is hard but important work, and it will be better if you have a follow-up plan that you stick to.

The Issue of Money

We live in a society that requires money for the necessities of life, and many of us feel we don't have enough. Most people experience money problems at some time in their lives. Living from paycheck to paycheck is a reality for lots of folks. Others are unemployed or underemployed and have limited resources. The pressure to make money affects everyone. For these reasons money can be a source of stress and conflict even in the healthiest relationships.

You may come into a relationship with more or less money than your partner, which can cause strain when you merge your lives and have bills to pay. One person may make more than the other, which can also influence saving and spending decisions. Couples may disagree about whether the money belongs to one person because he/she earned it or whether it's combined now that they're living together or married. If you are the sole provider (either by choice or because your partner is currently unemployed), do you have more of a say in how the money is spent?

In our domestic abuse groups, men often talk about how much money their female partners spend. The perception that women are spendthrifts and have no financial self-control often causes group participants to nod their heads in agreement. One man in our group was critical of what he perceived as his partner's excessive spending on clothes, but he saw no contradiction between his criticism of her and the money he spent on his motorcycle. Our values about spending may be different, but pointing fingers at each other over debt, savings, providing for children, and necessary purchases is not helpful. When couples are dishonest about money, problems can surface in a big way. *This is where your partnership comes in. Let's see how this works and how you might handle money problems in the future.*

EXERCISE 2 — Handling Money Problems

Complete this exercise if you and your partner get stuck in a disagreement about money. If you are not presently in a relationship, think about a money problem you had in a past relationship.

> Before beginning make sure you're in a quiet place where you won't be interrupted. Take some deep breaths to relax and clear your mind.

Part 1: Please review the following example exercise.

1. Describe as clearly, simply, and fairly as you can the money problem you are having.

   I think she's too uptight about money and blames me for our debt.

2. What do you think is your partner's perception of the problem?

   She thinks I'm not concerned enough about our financial problems and that I'm willing to spend money we don't have.

3. When and where do your partner and you usually argue about this issue? For example, what time of the week, day, or month? Do you argue on the phone, at home, in public?

   Usually at the end of the month when the bills have to be paid.

4. Do you think it is possible to reach a compromise that works for both of you?

   *Yes _____ No _____ Maybe _X_*

5. If yes or maybe, what can you safely do—without controlling, provoking, or blaming—to initiate a discussion in which your partner and you negotiate a solution to the conflict?
   Examples
   - *Discuss budgets and money commitments at the beginning of the month rather than when the bills are due and both people are anxious.*
   - *Discuss major projects or purchases that may need to be made during the year and attempt to reach agreement on priority items.*

6. If no, what can you do to handle this conflict safely over the long term?
   Examples
   - *I think we'll have to see a marriage counselor or a financial planner at some point because our values about money are so different.*
   - *Even though I disagree with her on this issue, I'm going to work on acknowledging her perspective.*

Part 2: Please answer the following questions.

1. Describe as clearly, simply, and fairly as you can the money problem you are having.

_____

_____

_____

2. What do you think is your partner's perception of the problem?

_____

_____

_____

3. When and where do your partner and you usually argue about this issue? For example, what time of the week, day, or month? Do you argue on the phone, at home, in public?

_____

_____

_____

4. Do you think it is possible to reach a compromise that works for both of you?
   Yes _____ No _____ Maybe _____

5. If yes or maybe, what can you safely do—without controlling, provoking, or blaming—to initiate a discussion in which your partner and you negotiate a solution to this conflict?

_____

_____

_____

6. If no, what can you do to handle this conflict safely over the long term?

_____

_____

_____

_____

Part 3: Please answer the following questions.

1. If you reached a compromise that both of you agreed to, return to this section in a month. Was the compromise successful? Yes _____ No _____

2. Does it need modification? If yes, describe the changes you will make in your plan to handle money problems.

_____

_____

_____

> If you're in a domestic abuse group, discuss this exercise together, preferably in small groups. Each participant should talk about what he learned from the exercise.

A Closing Thought

If your partner believes that the two of you can negotiate and compromise on money problems without fear of your acting out in an abusive manner, you and she can come to a cooperative arrangement. This might involve making a budget and sticking to it, talking to a counselor who specializes in money issues, and talking through your priorities on spending and saving. These issues don't have to be as complicated as we often make them. Regardless of your economic situation, working together with your partner to make ends meet is far more preferable—and successful—than working against each other.

Learning to Negotiate

Negotiating and compromising are important skills and are necessary for an intimate relationship to work. Couples always have disagreements and conflicts, but resolving differences doesn't have to be hurtful, and individuals certainly don't have to resort to abusive behavior to make their point.

A fair way to resolve conflicts in a relationship is to agree on a set of guidelines for discussing difficult issues. For men who have been violent in the past, this is crucial. Most men in our groups describe having an ongoing power struggle with their partners over certain issues. Because of your past behavior, it's important that you're fully committed to compromising and negotiating in a manner in which your partner can negotiate with you without any fears that you'll become violent or abusive.

Keep in mind that this isn't a labor or business negotiation. Nor are you like diplomats from two countries, trying to get the best possible arrangement using bargaining techniques designed to win. You are partners. You have a lot at stake here. Start from the perspective that you're both trying to improve your relationship or enhance your family. If you do, negotiations will go that much more smoothly.

Below is a fifteen-point guide your partner and you can use to help you resolve conflicts and problems fairly and respectfully. *Review the guide with your partner, and make sure you're both clear on these commitments.*

> **A Word of Caution:** If you are still in a relationship with a woman you have abused, she may not want to work on the same issues you do. She may not trust you. She may still harbor anger and resentment because of the abuse, and she may be confused about her feelings. She may still be afraid. The Negotiation Guide might not work right away for a woman who has been battered, and you shouldn't pressure her.

Negotiation Guide

1. Regardless of how angry or hurt I feel, I will remain nonviolent.
2. If I disagree with my partner's position, I will still be respectful toward her.
3. I will remain seated during the discussion.
4. I will not yell, scream, or use my voice in an intimidating manner.
5. I will not threaten my partner in any way.
6. I will not use put-downs, call my partner names, or be sarcastic or belittling.
7. I will not bring up past incidents to prove a point.
8. I will avoid blaming or shaming statements.
9. I will strive not to get defensive.
10. I will listen to my partner's position and refrain from interrupting.
11. I will commit to work toward a compromise.
12. I will be willing to explore my own issues and take responsibility for mistakes I have made.
13. I will respect my partner's wishes to end the discussion.
14. I will be honest.
15. I will talk about my feelings but will not use them as a way to manipulate my partner.

Before you begin: Before beginning negotiations on the issue you have disagreement on, settle on a good time to work on the problem. Make sure you have enough private time without interruptions from kids, jobs, or phones. Set a time limit, if necessary, so you can complete the process. Review the Negotiation Guide before you begin.

Listening: Now you're ready to start. One party states their position without being interrupted, regardless of how long it takes. Talk about the issue in detail, and express your feelings about it.

Example:

> *Our money situation is very troubling to me. I feel anxious because when the bills come, I'm not sure how we're going to make ends meet. We don't talk about priorities, and we both just spend, and then the bills are due. We seem to always end up in a huge fight, and we blame each other.*

Notice how there weren't any blaming statements in this example. This person has stated her position and her feelings. She's not proposing a solution at this point. Tell the other person when you're finished. The other person then states their understanding of the problem and explains their feelings.

After each of you has stated your positions, ask for clarification of each other's position if needed. For instance, you might want to say, "I want to be sure I understand the points you're making." See if you can restate her position. Now it's your partner's turn. It's important that you both understand each other's perspective.

Finding a solution: After you're both clear about the issue, one person can propose a solution. If you reach an impasse, try brainstorming some possible solutions. You don't have to reach a consensus right away. When you have reached an agreement, make sure that you're both clear about the resolution.

Example:

> *We have agreed that we will find a sample budget format online and use it to help us work up a budget listing the expenditures that are necessary on a monthly basis (rent, utilities, insurance, medical, transportation, groceries, etc.). We agree that any discretionary money left over after paying the bills will be prioritized and discussed on Fridays of each week. We will let each other know what personal or joint financial necessities are required, and we will jointly make a plan.*

Revisit the issue again to see how it's working. If there are still problems, you'll have to renegotiate. If your resolution is working, acknowledge the positive results that came out of negotiating fairly.

Committing to Fair Discussion

Negotiating through problems is important. Equally important is being able discuss day-to-day issues that require similar communication skills based on respect. In the past you may have used threats or coercion to get your way. You may have stood in the doorway so your partner couldn't leave, taken her car keys, pressured her to drop charges or a protection order, threatened to divorce her, warned her that you would get custody of the children, or told her you'd hurt her if she didn't change.

Hopefully at this stage in your domestic abuse group and after completing the exercises so far in this workbook, you've made commitments to change. Assuming your partner was willing to apply the tools in the Negotiation Guide, you've both experienced the positive results of compromising and resolving problems in an equitable manner. Being fair on a consistent basis also requires the willingness to accept change, accepting your partner's needs and wants, letting go of absolutes ("my way or the highway"), being flexible, respecting your partner's individuality, and communicating in a fair manner.

In our busy and often chaotic days, it's easy to become short with one another. The kids could be arguing, something breaks in the house, an appointment is missed—myriad problems can create tension. A comment, request, or question can be taken out of context, and an argument ensues. Before engaging in argument, commit to stepping back, taking a deep breath, and having a fair discussion about the issue or about how you and your partner are interacting.

Because of your past history of abuse it's important that you set high standards for yourself. If your partner says something hurtful or inappropriate during a discussion, it isn't necessary for you to match her. Once you take that step, you begin to slide down the slippery slope of not caring what you say and do, and you may become abusive.

Mark, a participant in our groups, described how a simple disagreement escalated into his abusing his wife:

> *The first time I was arrested for a domestic assault we were driving home and she wanted to get something to eat, but I refused to stop. We argued all the way home. She kept saying how I always got my way. We got home, and she said something derogatory to me. I grabbed her and pushed her into the wall. I was in a rage, and she was totally shocked at what I had done.*
>
> *She called the police. I really went off—I took the wedding pictures off the wall and smashed them on the floor. I was swearing and breaking other things in the house. She went to another room hoping that I would calm down. I grabbed a couple of knives from the kitchen and threw them at the wall, partly out of just being pissed and partly to scare her.*

Settling differences requires three basic things:

1. the desire to listen to the other person

2. the willingness to compromise

3. the determination to work things out, regardless of how difficult the task

Sometimes we're so convinced of the correctness of our position that we build walls around ourselves. Or we may be hurt or offended by what the other person is saying, and our response is to hurt back. Being able to listen to another person's feelings and thoughts on an issue is a skill worth possessing. It takes practice and determination.

Like the rules for negotiating, having a fair discussion requires certain commitments to an evenhanded and nonabusive communication process. The Fair Discussion Guide, below, is primarily for you, but you can also share it with your partner. She may agree that this plan could be useful for resolving problems. But remember, if you are still in a relationship with the woman you've abused, don't pressure her to use this guide. Discuss the matter with your counselor. Be open to having your counselor or a victim advocate talk with your partner about how these guides are being used. You can benefit from following the guidelines even if your partner doesn't use them.

The Fair Discussion Guide shares some similarities with the Negotiation Guide but is designed as a guiding light for your everyday communication with your partner. *Even if you're not in a relationship, see if these guidelines might work for you in the future.*

Fair Discussion Guide

Before you begin: Review these guidelines together, and add any that you both decide are important.

- Acknowledge that a fair discussion requires two people who are ready to talk. Don't force a discussion.

- Reminder: You know each other's weak spots. Don't use them to hurt your partner.

- Before you begin a discussion, you must first be committed to a fair process.

- Define the problem—it may be different for each person. What is negotiable? How does each person perceive and define the problem? Who else will be affected and how?

- Agree to deal with one issue at a time.

- Agree on how long you want to discuss the issue—you don't need to resolve everything in one sitting.

Try to:

- Listen. Try to understand what the other person is saying.

- Hear things you disagree with or find painful without reacting defensively.

- Use "I" statements, like "I think" or "I feel."

- Take responsibility for your past actions.

- Be honest.

- Be willing to apologize or state that you are willing to work on an issue.

- Encourage your partner to take equal time to present her position, as well as time to change her mind.

- Work toward a mutually satisfying solution.

- Accept that some things may need to change.

Try not to:

- Interrupt when your partner is talking.

- Raise your voice (for men who have battered, you need to be especially careful with your body language, tone of voice, looks, rolling of eyes, etc.).

- Blame your partner.

- Bring up the past to make your point.

- Walk away from the discussion.

- Make threats.

- Use other people's opinions to make your point.

Before you end the discussion:

- Each person should try to summarize what was stated.

- What was agreed to?

- What have you personally committed to?

- What still needs work?

- Can you agree to short-term and long-term goals?

- What needs to be part of an immediate and then a final solution? If a compromise is needed, list several long-term solutions you both think are fair.

- How did you feel about the discussion process? What improvements would you make in the future?

Reaching a Compromise

To help evaluate how you've handled conflicts in the past and how you might handle them in the future, complete the following exercise. While doing so, think about what you've learned from the Negotiation Guide and Fair Discussion Guide. Even if you are not in a relationship today, think about an incident in a past relationship when you could have reached a compromise with your partner but instead tried to control the situation by becoming abusive.

Reaching a Compromise

Before beginning make sure you're in a quiet place where you won't be interrupted. Take some deep breaths to relax and clear your mind.

Part 1: Please review the following example exercise.

1. Write down an incident when you became abusive during a disagreement.

   We argue about money a lot. There were a bunch of charges on our credit card, and I confronted her. She claimed we needed everything she'd charged. I told her I was going to cut up the cards unless she got some self-control. She told me to "fuck off," so I grabbed her purse, took the cards, and left.

2. Think about the way you handled the situation. Even though you were upset, how might you have reached a compromise in a fair and nonabusive manner?

   I shouldn't have brought up the issue when I was angry. I should have waited until I was calm and suggested a time to talk. We could have discussed the way we were both feeling about money, and I could have reassured her that I would not get upset. We could have both agreed to the points in the Fair Discussion Guide and the Negotiation Guide before discussing the issue.

Part 2: Please answer the following questions.

1. Write down an incident when you became abusive during a disagreement.

   _____

   _____

   _____

2. Think about the way you handled the situation. Even though you were upset, how might you have reached a compromise in a fair and nonabusive manner?

   _____

   _____

   _____

> If you're in a domestic abuse group, discuss this exercise together, preferably in small groups. Each participant should talk about what he learned from the exercise.

A Closing Thought

If your partner and you have made the decision to stay together, ideally (if your partner feels safe) you will both review the Negotiation and Fair Discussion Guides and agree that they are worthy tools. The principles in these guides really do work if you use them—but you have to use them more than just once in a while. Trying to use the rules and suggestions may at first seem a little awkward, but when you resolve a disagreement by negotiating fairly, discuss a contentious issue without being abusive, and reach an equitable compromise, you will feel better about your partner, yourself, and your relationship.

If you're not in a relationship now, think about whether the principles and rules in these guides might be applicable to you in a future relationship. In the past your habitual reaction to conflict may have been to simply lash out. If your partner said something you didn't like or did something that made you angry, you were ready for battle. You know there is a better way. In a new relationship you can either use some of the principles of these guides to ensure you don't fall back into old abusive patterns or share the guides with your new partner. If you're honest about your past with your new partner, she will probably welcome your pledge to be nonabusive with her and your commitment to being in a respectful partnership.

Developing a Personal Responsibility Plan

A Personal Responsibility Plan is your benchmark for the changes you've made and are continuing to make. It is a working document that you (individually or with help from your domestic abuse group) use to keep a record of your change process. You've now made the commitment to be nonviolent and nonabusive, but how will you ensure that you are putting into practice all that you've learned? There are three basic components to creating your Personal Responsibility Plan:

- **Commitment:** What are you willing to commit to doing differently?
- **Accountability:** How and to whom will you be accountable for past and future behavior?
- **Assessment:** How will you evaluate the progress you have made?

Commitment

If you have completed all or most of the exercises in this workbook, you have already done a fairly thorough evaluation of past situations in which you were abusive or violent with your partner. By now you recognize that you always had alternatives. You acknowledge that you've made some bad choices, and you probably wish you could go back and change history. Obviously you can't, but what happens when similar issues and conflicts come up today, especially if you're still in a relationship with the woman you abused? How will you deal with disagreement?

How will you interact with your partner without being abusive and controlling? How will you manage the negative emotions that may lie just below the surface? Who will you turn to when you need help to ensure that you honor your commitment to your partner and to yourself to stay nonviolent?

This exercise will help you outline a plan for handling disagreements and arguments with your partner. *Let's examine how you can fulfill your commitment to staying nonviolent and non-abusive. If you're not in a relationship now, think about applying these commitments in a future relationship.*

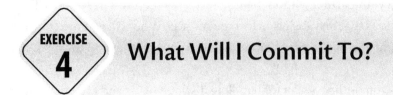

What Will I Commit To?

Before beginning make sure you're in a quiet place where you won't be interrupted. Take some deep breaths to relax and clear your mind.

Part 1: Please review the following example exercise.

1. Write down several areas of conflict that have presented the most difficulty for you in the past.

   - I get angry and defensive when my partner criticizes me.
   - I don't like the way she disciplines our son.
   - She says things in public or at parties that I think are embarrassing.
   - I think she doesn't manage our money well.

2. Write down ten concrete steps you will take to ensure that you respond nonabusively when a similar disagreement arises again with your partner.

   - If I think I'll become abusive, I will take a time-out.
   - I will think about what my partner has said rather than rehearsing how I am going to respond to her.
   - I will not use violence or any abusive behaviors against my partner.
   - I will work on my problems with my partner and commit to the principles in the Negotiation and Fair Discussion Guides.
   - I will work on letting go of always wanting to control situations.
   - I will commit to an exercise program to reduce stress.
   - I will use positive self-talk when I'm getting upset.
   - I will take responsibility for my behavior.
   - I will expand my support network when I get out of counseling.
   - I will go back into counseling if I need help with issues.

Part 2: Please answer the following questions.

1. Write down several areas of conflict that have presented the most difficulty for you in the past.

_____

_____

_____

2. Write down ten concrete steps you will take to ensure that you respond nonabusively when a similar disagreement arises again with your partner.

_____

_____

_____

_____

_____

> If you're in a domestic abuse group, discuss this exercise together, preferably in small groups. Each participant should talk about what he learned from the exercise.

Accountability

If we are serious about making amends for past behavior and ensuring that we don't repeat past mistakes, we have to do more than just apologize.

If you have battered an intimate partner, accountability means you are answerable to your partner, to your children who observed the violence, to other people who have been affected by your violence—including friends, family members, counselors, and group members—and to yourself. This can be hard.

Promises that the behavior won't happen again are insufficient. The idea of accountability is that the person who caused the harm will take certain steps to provide assurances that the behavior won't recur, which requires a plan. This is an important process. Even if you make efforts to be accountable, your partner may still have legitimate mistrust. Give her time, and make these commitments because it's the right thing to do. _Let's examine how you can be accountable to your partner. If you're not in a relationship now, what does accountability mean for your children or in a future relationship?_

Being and Staying Accountable

> Before beginning make sure you're in a quiet place where you won't be interrupted. Take some deep breaths to relax and clear your mind.

Part 1: Please review the following example exercise.

1. List the people you believe you should talk to about your past use of violence and your future goals of being nonviolent.

   My wife, Annie; my ten-year-old daughter, Caroline; and my mother-in-law, Sara.

2. Outline what you want to say to each person to be accountable for your past and future. Set a date to talk to each person.

   To Annie, I will acknowledge that I am solely responsible for my past use of violence. I will discuss with her how I rationalized what I did. I will admit that my abuse was wrong. I will tell her that I understand that she may be distrustful because of my past behavior. I will apologize. I will tell her that I'm committed to being nonviolent and that I will follow some of what I am learning from the exercises in this workbook and in my counseling groups. I will talk to her on [date].

   To Caroline, I will apologize for hurting her mother. I will explain to her that what I did was wrong and that there is no excuse for my behavior. I will tell her that I've learned a lot about myself through counseling. I will promise to never be abusive to anyone in the family. I will apologize for putting her in the position of having to witness my violence and abusive behavior. I will tell her that I hope I can win back her trust. I will talk to her on [date].

   To Sara, I will acknowledge that I am responsible for my past use of violence. I will admit that what I did was wrong. I will tell her that I understand that she may be distrustful because of what I did to her daughter. I will also apologize for being defensive and verbally abusive to her when she confronted me about my behavior. I will tell her that I'm committed to being nonviolent. I will also tell her that I will go back to counseling if I start reverting to my old ways. I will talk to her on [date].

Part 2: Please answer the following questions.

1. List the people you believe you should talk to about your past use of violence and your future goals of being nonviolent.

_____

_____

_____

_____

2. Outline what you want to say to each person to make yourself accountable for your past and future. Set a date to talk to each person. Use an additional piece of paper if necessary for this step.

_____

_____

_____

_____

_____

_____

> If you're in a domestic abuse group, discuss this exercise together, preferably in small groups. Each participant should talk about what he learned from the exercise.

Assessment

How will you evaluate whether your changes are making a difference? How will you know if some of your actions have had unintended consequences? You will need some honest feedback. Before asking your partner for feedback, you need to have a way to measure the things that have changed and the areas that still need improvement. If you are still in a group, ask your counselor or facilitator how long you should wait before assessing your progress. Some men may want to assess their progress every three months; for others, a six-month assessment period makes more sense.

This assessment is for your benefit. If your partner doesn't want to participate, honor her request. If she does participate, you may hear things that make you feel uncomfortable. Remember your commitment. Trust the feedback you are receiving. This is a long-term process, and, despite your efforts, everything you want to happen won't just magically occur. *Let's examine how you can concretely assess your progress.*

Assessing Your Progress

Before beginning make sure you're in a quiet place where you won't be interrupted. Take some deep breaths to relax and clear your mind.

Part 1: Please review the following example exercise.

1. Review the ten steps you committed to in Exercise 4 above.

2. In the past three or six months, how would you rate the amount of progress you have made toward achieving your goals? If your partner is willing, ask her to also give her impressions of your actions. After each commitment, give yourself a letter grade, and comment briefly.

   a) I will not use violence or any abusive behaviors against my partner.
      I wasn't violent, but I slammed a door during a disagreement.   **C**

   b) I will take a time-out when I feel agitated, and I will follow the time-out rules.
      I have taken three time-outs, but one time I didn't let her know my plans.   **B**

   c) I will work on my problems with my partner and commit to the rules in the Negotiation Guide and Fair Discussion Guide.
      I tried to negotiate fairly, but Donna said I was being manipulative.   **C**

   d) I will work on letting go of always wanting to control situations.
      I still want things done the way I want them and get upset when they're not.   **C–**

   e) I will commit to an exercise program to reduce stress.
      I've been working out after work and feeling less stressed.   **A–**

   f) I will use positive self-talk when I'm getting upset.
      I have a hard time pushing negative stuff out of my mind.   **C**

   g) I will take responsibility for my behavior.
      When I've been upset and my behavior has been scary, I've acknowledged it and apologized.   **B**

   h) I will expand my support network when I get out of counseling.
      Except for the group, I haven't talked to anyone about my problems.   **D**

   i) I will go back into counseling if I need help with issues.
      I haven't needed to go back to counseling.

   j) I will work on having a more equal relationship with my partner.
      I am more aware of when I'm being controlling.   **C+**

Part 2: Please answer the following questions.

1. Review the ten concrete steps you committed to in Exercise 4 above.

2. In the past three or six months, how would you rate the amount of progress you have made toward achieving your goals? If your partner is willing, ask her to also give impressions of your actions. After each commitment, give yourself a letter grade and comment briefly. If necessary, use additional paper for this step.

_____

_____

_____

_____

_____

_____

_____

> If you're in a domestic abuse group, discuss this exercise together, preferably in small groups. Each participant should talk about what he learned from the exercise.

A Closing Thought

If you are still in your domestic abuse program, you might want to review your assessment report with your counselor or other group members. It is important to generate some ideas on how you might improve in certain areas, so feedback is valuable. If you seriously and genuinely adhere to the three components of a Personal Responsibility Plan—commitment, accountability, and assessment—you will not only realize noticeable changes; you will also have a sense of security that your new life is heading down the right path.

Healing

For men who have battered, healing involves many parts. Taking full responsibility for your past use of violence is usually a difficult process, but it *is* part of healing. You may have been arrested or had a civil protection order taken out against you. Or perhaps you volunteered to participate in a domestic abuse group because your violence has caused such pain and turmoil. If you are beyond the stage where you are blaming your partner or rationalizing your use of violence (which most men who batter do), the only thing left is to look at yourself squarely in the mirror and ask some fairly big life questions.

- How did I get to this place?
- How do I ensure that I won't abuse an intimate partner in the future?
- How can I make amends for my past behavior?
- How do I apply what I've learned so I can have a relationship with my current or future partner that is based on respect, trust, love, shared responsibilities, and equality?
- How can I live a more healthy and fulfilling life in the future?

Healing is a matter of time, but it's also a matter of opportunity.
— HIPPOCRATES

In this workbook you've analyzed your past violent behavior and explored how our sexist society helped to shape your attitudes and beliefs about women and intimate relationships. You've dissected past incidents in which you were violent and abusive by examining the purpose behind your actions. You know now that you didn't just "lose control" when you became violent. You better understand the impact of your abusive actions on your partner, your children, and yourself. You've looked at all of the ways you denied or downplayed the violence. You've also recognized that there were always alternatives to being violent.

By participating in your domestic abuse group and using this workbook, you now have many tools, guides, exercises, plans, and hopefully insights to help you change. But many twists and turns in your journey may still lie ahead.

Healing is the process of making ourselves whole—of restoring our physical, psychological, emotional, and spiritual health. Many men in our groups have co-occurring conditions. In other words, they have a problem with domestic abuse, but they also may have substance abuse addictions or other mental health issues. If you think you have other problems that aren't addressed in your domestic abuse group, ask the group counselors for a referral to see a therapist or substance abuse treatment center for an evaluation. If you're not in a group, there are plenty of resources in your community. (See the Resources section, located in the back of this workbook, for a list of some of them.)

Now is the time to take a serious inventory of the way you are currently living your life and assess what you still need to work on. Many of the men whom I interviewed in the book *Violent No More* stayed nonviolent because they recognized that they had been living their lives out of balance on many levels. They didn't just complete their domestic abuse groups and walk out the door. Some of them went into treatment, got counseling, attended support groups, read books, and continued to make changes in their lives.

As Ron said:

> I'm committed to not being violent or abusive with Anne. I'd like to believe that all of my abuse is in the past, but I still don't totally trust myself. Fifteen years after getting ordered into counseling, I know I still have issues with women and relationships. A few years back I went into therapy for a long time to work on my childhood stuff. It was hard and painful, but I learned a lot about myself. That experience was important to me.
>
> I think about my violent history and about the kinds of struggles men and women have in relationships, and I try to understand how my past has influenced me today. As long as I continue to talk about these issues and as long as my thinking is challenged, I know I'll be okay. It's about awareness and remembering where you were, and, of course, how you want to live your life in the present and in the future.

Dave also described some of the changes that took place in his partnership:

> Almost every day when we get off work, Kris and I have coffee and discuss our day. We talk about money, the kids, work, our relationship—we make sure we have this special time. This is very different for me. In the past it was hard for me to communicate, especially talking about my fears and insecurities. I kept everything inside.
>
> I try to live my life in a way that keeps me in balance. I like that Kris and I are equal, and I like the way we communicate. I try to take care of myself emotionally and spiritually. I'll go to a powwow as part of my spiritual life, and I try to keep learning things by reading. I still go to AA. I've had heart problems, so I try to keep healthy physically, although that is an area that could stand some improvement.

Health and Balance

What does the concept of living your life in balance mean? We all have dreams and aspirations, but for many reasons we get sidetracked and develop habits that block us from reaching our full potential. There are no one-size-fits-all techniques for living your life in balance, but I hope this section (which is almost entirely excerpted from the book *Violent No More*) provides some perspective.

I first learned about the idea of living in balance and harmony from a native American man named Marlin Mousseau. Marlin grew up on the Pine Ridge Indian Reservation in South Dakota and now works with abusive men in Wisconsin. He developed Project Medicine Wheel, designed to help abusive men in the Native American community understand their use of violence, to motivate them to live in harmony and balance, and to use traditional Indian ways of healing.

Marlin states that an individual is made up of four essences: emotion, body, spirit, and mind (the intellectual side). If one of these areas is off, the person is out of balance and is not living in harmony with the world. I think men are frequently out of balance. Unfortunately we have little guidance or support for changing our unhealthy habits. The following are some thoughts on living in balance, adapted from Marlin's four essences.

The Emotional Side

Men in our groups often say they don't know how to talk on a truly emotional level. This is because like many men, they have been socialized not to talk about their feelings. Gradually they become afraid to show their true self, and their emotional side becomes disconnected from the whole. The longer men avoid expressing their feelings, the harder it becomes to change.

Occasionally I have chosen to withdraw in an intimate relationship by withholding my feelings or not talking about what is going on in my life. Sometimes I'll give just a hint of what's wrong. Every time I hold back, there's a consequence. I become more distant and the relationship suffers.

Men need to open up emotionally. We need to talk about what we're really feeling, and not just with our partners but with our friends, too—both women and men. People usually want to talk about their lives on a less superficial level, but they don't think they have permission to. We feel that if we open up, our friends, family members, or intimate partners will think there's something wrong with us, that we're too needy or self-absorbed. Talking on a deeper level takes practice, and it isn't a one-way street. You must also genuinely care about what the other person is saying, thinking, and feeling. Your concern and response will be reciprocated. You can just be there for each other without having to solve each other's problems.

The Physical Side

We would all benefit from being active, staying in shape, and putting the right nourishment into our bodies, but we often resist. Many of us are out of shape, which usually leads to physical problems as we age. Men often ignore health problems and overwork themselves, thinking they are invincible.

An exercise routine takes discipline. Exercise is not only good for the body, it is also emotionally uplifting. Yet there always seems to be something else to do or some excuse. I've often left work feeling I had absolutely no energy to exercise. All I wanted to do was to go home, watch something mindless on the TV, eat, and go to bed. If I force myself to go to the gym or for a run, I almost always enjoy the exercise and feel reinvigorated and glad I made the effort.

Balancing your physical side also requires monitoring what you put into your body. We hear how important it is to eat a healthy diet and eat in moderation, yet we frequently ignore the advice. Men especially think they can abuse their bodies without consequence. Many men think that cancer or heart disease will happen to someone else or that there's always time to change.

Search on the Internet or get a book for advice on maintaining a balanced and healthy diet. Eating more fruits and vegetables and less dairy, red meat, and sugar, reducing your intake of processed and fast foods, and eating in a balanced way will keep you healthier. You don't have to be overly rigid at every meal, but once you've eliminated certain foods from your diet, you won't miss them. Losing those extra pounds will make you feel better about yourself, too.

Some men continue to smoke despite the extensive medical evidence that tobacco use causes heart disease and cancer. Some engage in unsafe sex even though they know the risks of AIDS and other STIs. Some men drink to excess and consume dangerous drugs regardless of the physical and psychological effects. Some men believe they are indestructible. Don't make these mistakes. Choose to care about yourself instead!

If you are not involved in an exercise routine, commit to one now. Join a Y or an exercise club and find a routine that feels good and is fun. Buy some running shoes and walk, run, or jog. Play basketball, racquetball, soccer, baseball, or tennis. Lift weights, go biking, dance, practice yoga, or join a kick-boxing class. As the saying goes, just do it! Working out at least three days a week will keep your weight down, increase cardiovascular endurance, and make you feel better.

The Spiritual Side

When I mention the spiritual level, I am not referring to attending services at a church, temple, mosque, or other place of worship, although that may be where you find spiritual connection. Being spiritual can also mean getting in touch with the world around you. This feeling of connectedness can occur through meditating, walking in a park or in the woods, or sitting by a creek. Some people pray, chant, sing, or listen to music as a way of finding a source of spiritual light.

Several years ago I went to a retreat where I learned about meditation. We were asked to focus on the impermanence of life and the limited time we spend on the earth. I remember feeling sad during this meditation, a sadness that had much to do with my own feelings at the time. I was confused about the pain in the world and wondered about the purpose of my life. I had no answer. Today when I think back on that time and the focus on impermanence, I understand the message: In the short time we are here, we need to live our lives with significance and purpose. We do not necessarily have to do something earth shattering, just live with more compassion and love.

Although it is an important lesson, I often forget it. I choose to live a spiritually unbalanced life because the world around me seems so cold, unloving, and angry. The collective pain of families and communities spills out all around me. I easily become withdrawn, and I insulate myself by becoming cynical, self-absorbed, and uncaring. When the pain I see in my work overwhelms me, I know I am spiritually out of balance, and I know it's by my choice.

When I choose to slow down, put my life in perspective, and take the steps to reconnect with what is really important, my connection to the universe around me is strengthened. I often find this renewal in the woods, near a lake or river, in the mountains, or in the sky on a starry night. We can all find our peace.

The Intellectual Side

On the intellectual level, many of us men have a difficult time being open to new ideas. We get locked into a certain way of thinking and refuse to hear opposing views. Listen, for example, to other men discussing politics or even sports. The debate becomes almost warlike, with each person determined to win. I'm not suggesting that we be afraid to debate or give up principled positions. But when we refuse to listen to other ideas, we become hardened and cynical.

You don't have to be a rocket scientist to nurture your mind. Simply be open to information and ideas. Allow yourself time to reflect. To broaden your intellectual horizons, take a class, read books or newspapers, join an organization in which ideas are shared, or volunteer in your community.

Circle of Balance

How well balanced is your day-to-day life right now?
What parts of your life need your attention?
How can you make that right?

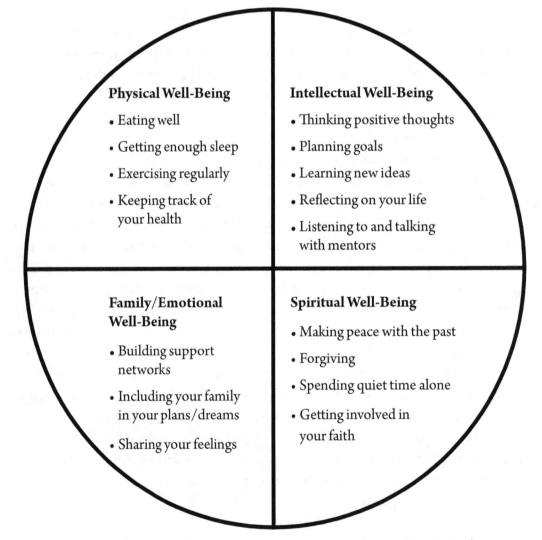

Physical Well-Being

- Eating well
- Getting enough sleep
- Exercising regularly
- Keeping track of your health

Intellectual Well-Being

- Thinking positive thoughts
- Planning goals
- Learning new ideas
- Reflecting on your life
- Listening to and talking with mentors

Family/Emotional Well-Being

- Building support networks
- Including your family in your plans/dreams
- Sharing your feelings

Spiritual Well-Being

- Making peace with the past
- Forgiving
- Spending quiet time alone
- Getting involved in your faith

(Adapted from a model by Rose Pere, a Maori woman from Aotearoa/New Zealand)

Unfortunately, television and other electronic media have become the dominant sources of ideas and information for many people, replacing books and the discussion of opinions and beliefs with family members, friends, and neighbors. The vast array of technology at our disposal and our constant use of social media have made life more complex and less personal. It seems like everyone is glued to their electronic devices, feeling compelled to see who has communicated messages, commentary, and news. Our political discourse has become increasingly toxic; people don't have to take responsibility for comments they can make anonymously. Our news media are highly partisan; programs speak to their political base without a thoughtful analysis. We make our own choices about how we participate in this high-tech era. We can choose to be lifelong learners with curiosity and openness about new ideas, or we can settle for sound bites about our community and the events in the world.

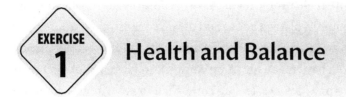

EXERCISE 1 — Health and Balance

Review the Circle of Balance, above. It provides a visual framework for finding health and balance. In this exercise you'll be asked to evaluate your current status in each of the four areas. Doing so can help you determine what steps you might want to take to live a more balanced life.

> Before beginning make sure you're in a quiet place where you won't be interrupted. Take some deep breaths to relax and clear your mind.

Part 1: Please review the following example exercise.

1. Briefly explain how you feel today about the state of each of the following essences (categories) in your life. Doing well? Needs improvement? If you're lacking in any of the four essences, list the specific deficiencies. Why do you think you're having problems with that particular essence?

Emotional/Family

Needs improvement. My family situation has been in turmoil. My violence obviously has caused a lot of problems. I volunteered for this domestic abuse program because I think Kelly is going to leave me. I keep telling her I'll change, but she's still scared of me, and the kids are, too. I try talking to my friends, but I feel pretty stuck and bummed out.

Physical

Doing well. I have a group of guys that I play basketball with twice a week, so I get a lot of exercise, and I'm in fairly good shape. I probably drink too much, but I try to eat healthy.

Spiritual

Needs improvement. I'm not religious. I can't stop thinking about this mess I'm in, although I am committed to change. I haven't decided what to do. I have this empty feeling about the future.

Intellectual

Doing well. As depressing as all of my family stuff is, I'm really trying to be honest about what's going on in my life. I want to change, and I know my abuse has damaged my wife, my kids, and myself. I'm learning a lot in this group.

2. List some things you can do differently to bring these parts of your life into better balance.

Emotional/Family

I'm going to continue to work on what I've learned in the groups. I know my relationship is on shaky ground, but I need to change for me. I'm hoping my kids will see that I'm changing and not be nervous about my having mood swings.

Physical

I'm going to continue working out. I'm going to try to cut down on my drinking.

Spiritual

Some of the guys in the group have talked about what they've learned in counseling. I'm going to make an appointment with a counselor.

Intellectual

I'm going to continue thinking positively about this change process I'm in. I'm reading the materials that I get in my groups and using the exercises in this workbook.

Part 2: Please answer the following questions.

1. Briefly explain how you feel today about the state of each of the following essences (categories) in your life. Doing well? Needs improvement? If you're lacking in any of the four essences, list the specific deficiencies. Why do you think you're having problems with that particular essence?

Emotional/Family

_____

_____

_____

_____

_____

Physical

_____

_____

_____

_____

Spiritual

_____

_____

_____

_____

Intellectual

_____

_____

_____

_____

2. List some things you can do differently to bring these parts of your life into better balance.

Emotional/Family

_____

_____

_____

Physical

_____

_____

_____

Spiritual

_____

_____

_____

Intellectual

_____

_____

_____

> If you're in a domestic abuse group, discuss this exercise together, preferably in small groups. Each participant should talk about what he learned from the exercise.

A Closing Thought

There is a concept in Eastern spiritual practice called "mindfulness." It basically means living your life in the present and not being overly consumed with the past or the future. This concept isn't a contradiction to what you been learning. It's important that we learn from our past mistakes, but we also have to live in the moment. Your future will evolve if you live your life in a more peaceful manner. Pay attention to your physical, emotional, intellectual, and spiritual sides, and you'll see changes in your life and in the people who are close to you. You've learned a lot so far in your journey, but don't stop now.

As mentioned, most men know the risks of unhealthy behavior, but many shrug them off, either believing that they won't get sick or exhibiting a fatalistic (macho) façade about life, as in, "Hey, we all gotta go sometime." This attitude is unfair to your family and to yourself.

Many (but certainly not all) men in our domestic abuse groups will tell us that they enjoyed the groups and that they learned a lot about themselves. Sadly, however, when they leave the group they become isolated and no longer have a safe place to talk about personal issues and the struggles they are having with their change process. The commitments they made to living healthier lifestyles slip away, and imbalance sets in again. Don't let this happen. Stay committed to the goals you've set for yourself. Ask for help—you'll be glad you did.

Staying on Course: A Lifelong Commitment

Most of the men I interviewed for the book *Violent No More* told me they continually work to avoid reverting to old behaviors. They had made commitments to change, and many said they used the information they learned in our groups to stay nonviolent and nonabusive. But many men admitted it was a struggle. Whenever they feel hurt, jealous, or angry, their first thoughts are to react in a way that will get them what they want. Being intimidating was so much a part of how they handled conflict in the past that it remains almost an automatic reaction. Yelling or grabbing their partners would make their partners afraid and put them on the defensive. If the partners resisted, the men could always resort to more violence.

Earl, a man in one of my groups, talked about the challenge of staying on course:

> *I had promised my wife, Kathy, that I would never hit her again. I really made an effort to apply the things I'd learned in my group and the self-control techniques I'd worked on. I was determined not to repeat my past behavior. We were having an argument about something, and I leaned across the table and yelled, "Now you listen!" She was really startled, and I was kind of shocked that I did it. I felt the same rush I used to feel when I battered her, and I was aware of her fear. I saw how easy it would be for me to slip back into old behaviors.*

I have seen men in our domestic abuse programs make profound changes. Andy was ordered into our groups by the courts and like a lot of men was very resistant at first. But over time his attitude shifted:

After four or five group sessions something happened for me. It was actually free-ing to take responsibility for my own behavior. It was challenging to examine my beliefs. I began to enjoy going to groups and talking about this stuff with other men. Even though I started making changes, it wasn't enough to save my rela-tionship with Debra. I guess too much had happened between us—too much pain and too much of my violence—for us to heal as a couple.

Rather than getting into a rebound relationship, Andy continued on his change process. He went to counseling to work on his family of origin issues, attended college, got his degree, and stayed sober. He started facilitating domestic abuse groups at our program and got remarried. Andy fully understood that he could revert to old patterns even after everything he'd learned:

During those first two years of marriage, when Beth and I would argue, I would sometimes get sarcastic and raise my voice, and at other times I would just shut down and withdraw. I would usually apologize when I was acting in an inappro-priate manner. This was a painful time for both of us.

Andy and Beth struggled and even separated for a short period. He went to counseling on his own, and then they both went into marriage counseling. They didn't give up. Andy had a reservoir of knowledge about domestic abuse and relationship dynamics, but even he didn't fully recognize how his past could haunt him. One day, during a conversation when Beth was being honest with Andy, he realized he needed to do more to meet his lifelong commitment to staying nonviolent:

Beth told me there were times she was scared of me. I couldn't believe it. She would say, "You know, you're a big guy, and when we get into an argument, if you raise your voice, it makes me afraid sometimes." She would then qualify these statements by saying, "I don't believe you'll physically hurt me, but I still feel afraid." I never sensed she felt this way, because she wouldn't shut down or retreat from any conflicts we were having. When she confronted me about this, it really floored me. I didn't want to own it, I didn't want to entertain it, I didn't want to feel it, and I didn't want to hear it. I so desperately didn't want her to be afraid of me, but she was.

Here I was, working with men who batter, and I'm very visible in the commu-nity because of my work, and here Beth is telling me that sometimes she's fearful. It was really depressing. All I had ever wanted was to be a loving husband to Beth and a loving stepparent to the kids. I wanted her to love me, approve of me, and think I'm somebody special. So when she told me about being scared, I felt like a monster. I hated it.

Andy religiously used the tools he had learned from his domestic abuse group and the knowledge he shared with other men who batter when he was facilitating groups. He would be the first to say that not only do you need to stick to your commitments, but you must be open to feedback without getting defensive.

Check in with your partner. How does she feel about the way you're dealing with the inevi-table conflicts that occur in a relationship? Are you using any abusive behaviors either to get your way or as a punishment?

Whether it's fair or not, men who have battered need honest feedback. Your current or future partner may wonder if you'll lapse into using undesirable behaviors when you're having relationship problems. Eventually such fears slowly dissipate as trust grows.

The rewards of sticking to your lifelong commitment are immeasurable. As Andy said about his marriage now:

> Beth and I have a great relationship today. She's my best friend. We have a level of intimacy that's very special. As I said the first two years were a struggle, but we worked things through. I believe if those kinds of problems surfaced again, we would recognize the signs and deal with the issues in a heartbeat. This comes from a deeper level of commitment to our relationship that simply wasn't there those first two years of our marriage. We often talk about our relationship and how far we've come. There have been times when we just hold each other, and we're brought to tears because of how deep our love and intimacy are today. We have created a process for checking things out with each other. The love and respect that we have for each other are very powerful.

The exercises in this workbook have challenged you to look back at events in your life. By writing down the thoughts and feelings you had at the time, you can measure what you've learned and how you might handle similar situations today. Hopefully you've had a meaningful discussion about these issues in a domestic abuse group.

Let's review what you've learned and how you will stick to your lifelong commitment to remaining nonviolent and nonabusive with an intimate partner.

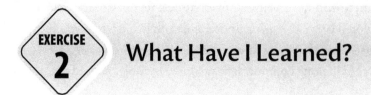

What Have I Learned?

Before beginning make sure you're in a quiet place where you won't be interrupted. Take some deep breaths to relax and clear your mind.

Please answer the following questions.

1. How did you learn about violence as a young person?

_____

_____

_____

2. Where did your beliefs about women, men, masculinity, and intimate relationships come from?

_____

_____

_____

3. What does the term "battering" mean to you?

_____

_____

_____

4. Why has it been difficult to take responsibility for your behavior?

_____

_____

_____

_____

5. What have you committed to changing in your life?

_____

_____

_____

6. Where do you need to focus your energies in your change process? What steps will you take next?

_____

_____

_____

> If you're in a domestic abuse group, discuss this exercise together, preferably in small groups. Each participant should talk about what he learned from the exercise.

A Closing Note

People continually battle with the commitments they've made to improve their lives. This is understandable. We should set our sights high, and plenty of advice is out there to help you do so. Bookstores—both brick-and-mortar and online—have entire sections featuring self-improvement books on how to make more money, plan for retirement, seek a good-paying job, enhance your sexual experiences, be more assertive, communicate with your children, and improve your health. Your commitment to end your domestic abuse, however, goes way beyond reading a self-help book or attending a domestic abuse group, although both are important.

Change is an ongoing process. At first you may not get much support from your friends or family. Like an alcoholic who quits drinking, people who observed past episodes of intoxication or inappropriate behavior may be uncertain about whether to trust the changes you've made. Your friends or family may still be on the alert for outbursts, angry body language, sarcasm, and other abusive behaviors that they witnessed in the past. Still you will know that your new path is the right one.

> **A Note of Caution:** Some female partners of the men in our groups have stated that their husbands or boyfriends used the new language (some might call it "group-speak") they learned in their domestic groups or in counseling against them. For instance, men might say to their partners, "I'm not being aggressive, I'm just being assertive." "Why are you asking me where I'm going? You're trying to isolate me." "You're the one who is using the abusive behaviors on the Power and Control Wheel." "You're minimizing your actions."
>
> Knowledge is power. If you are using (abusing) any of your newfound information about domestic abuse or relationships as a way to control your partner or justify inappropriate behavior, you're really not committed to changing.

EXERCISE 3 — Building a Support System

If you are nearing the completion of your domestic abuse program, you have learned a lot about yourself. You now have the information you need to remain nonviolent and nonabusive with an intimate partner. The question is whether you can sustain what you've learned when conflicts surface, because they inevitably will.

My colleague Graham Barnes has worked extensively with men who batter in New Zealand and the United States. He conducts an exercise with men who are completing their group sessions. If you are in a group, your counselor may use this exercise (or something similar) to stress the importance of having a good support system to help you honor your commitments. If you're not in a group, you can still complete the exercise; it will give you some insights into who can help you stay nonviolent.

Graham explains that when things are going well, we don't have much need for a support system. But when life becomes difficult, it's important to turn to people we trust and to pursue activities that will keep us in balance, as described earlier in this chapter. The following is a variation on Graham's exercise.

> Before beginning make sure you're in a quiet place where you won't be interrupted. Take some deep breaths to relax and clear your mind.

Part 1: Please review the following example exercise.

1. List some people you might turn to in order to help you remain nonviolent and nonabusive. These are people you can be honest with and who will give you helpful feedback.

   - *close friends*
   - *family members*
   - *my partner (Note: your partner may not be helpful in this situation, because the feelings you are experiencing and the issues that are causing conflict may be related to her.)*
   - *my AA sponsor*
   - *someone from this domestic abuse group*
   - *a person from my faith community*

2. List resources or activities that you could draw on in a crisis, especially if your issues or problems are related to your backsliding into abusive behaviors and attitudes in your relationship.

- *reviewing exercises in this workbook*
- *reading books that provide perspective on life and relationships*
- *doing exercises that reduce stress*
- *meditation or prayer*
- *talking to my AA sponsor*
- *going to a counselor*
- *staying in my domestic abuse group, even if I've completed it*
- *sitting in a park, walking on a trail, canoeing on a lake, or being in a place where I find peace*

Part 2: Please answer the following questions.

1. List some people you might turn to in order to help you remain nonviolent and non-abusive. These are people you can be honest with and who will give you helpful feedback.

_____

_____

_____

_____

_____

2. List resources or activities that you could draw on in a crisis, especially if your issues or problems are related to your backsliding into negative behaviors and attitudes in your relationship.

_____

_____

_____

3. Write down three things you will commit to doing to build a support system for yourself.

_____

_____

_____

_____

4. Write down three things you could do to support other men in your group or friends who find themselves with similar problems.

_____

_____

_____

_____

5. Return to this exercise in thirty days. Who did you seek out for support or feedback about issues in your life? What activities did you pursue to help you when you were feeling isolated, confused, angry, or sad? How did you help other men in your group or friends who were struggling with similar problems?

_____

_____

_____

_____

> If you're in a domestic abuse group, discuss this exercise together, preferably in small groups. Each participant should talk about what he learned from the exercise.

A Closing Thought

Many men we've worked with have told us that they don't have a good support system. They might feel uncomfortable talking with friends or family members about relationship issues, their feelings, or their past use of violence. Some men don't have close friends. Some men don't read books or practice ways to relax and be reflective. For many men the only person they typically go to when they are troubled is their partner. As stated, if you find yourself in this situation, your partner may be the very *last* person you should go to when you're in a crisis—especially if you have unresolved problems with her.

You don't have to face your problems alone. If you are in a domestic abuse group, the other men can help you, and you can help them. Some men think it's a sign of weakness to seek help from a counselor. It isn't. You have to overcome the barriers to change that you have put in place. Take some risks by building new relationships with people who will support you in meaningful ways—and not just tell you what you want to hear.

Getting Men and Boys Engaged with Ending Gender Violence

Support for Changing Men

How is it possible that in the twenty-first century, every year tens of thousands of women and girls are victims of horrendous gendered-based crimes such as sexual assaults, trafficking, intimate partner homicides, honor killings, gang rapes, and genital mutilation? How is it possible that even with all of the changes in our laws and in the public's awareness, men's violence against women is still so commonplace? How has men's violence against women become so normalized?

Revelations about domestic abuse in the National Football League, sexual assaults in the military, and rape on college campuses will hopefully open up a long-needed dialogue about how to address men's violence against women. Of the 771 arrests of NFL players since 2000, at least 116 were related to domestic abuse. Annually there are over three thousand *reported* sexual assaults in the military, with the actual number estimated at closer to nineteen thousand. Not all of the victims of sexual assault in the military are female, but the vast majority of perpetrators are men. The number of reported rapes at four-year colleges increased 49 percent between 2008 and 2012. Some of these higher numbers are attributed to victims being more willing to come forward with their stories. Nevertheless, the numbers are startling, and as men we must be part of the conversation and part of the solution.

> *Sexual, racial, gender violence and other forms of discrimination and violence cannot be eliminated without changing culture.*
> — CHARLOTTE BUNCH

As you certainly know, addressing one's personal issues with domestic abuse is hard work. Even more challenging is coming to terms with the reality that men's violence against women is so widespread internationally. Some men (and even some women) become defensive about a summary of statistics that identifies so many men as perpetrators in domestic abuse and sexual assault cases. "Men's rights" organizations challenge assumptions made about gender violence and claim that a "feminist agenda" aims to indict all men. They assert that women are as violent as men. Although some women are perpetrators, the number of women raping or beating men pales in comparison to the number of men abusing and assaulting women. Women's violence against men is simply not a social problem like men's violence against women.

These are hard issues to talk about, but we can't deny the historical reality of men's violence against women. We can remain silent and pretend that the problem doesn't exist or that it's not *our* responsibility to fix. But you are now aware that men's violence against women is a huge problem, and that as men we need to step up. It may seem counterintuitive to say so, but your personal experiences with domestic abuse can give you some added credibility when you talk with men and boys about gender violence. As a changing man you can speak with conviction when you challenge men and boys to explore how our sexist society shapes men's behavior and their beliefs in male entitlement. You now have insight into how our culture influenced you to objectify and control women. Your personal history, awareness, and change process can be a powerful story.

No matter how you define your own masculinity, being a man doesn't mean you have to be sexist or support sexism. Men who are comfortable with their masculinity don't feel the need to defend sexist beliefs and locker-room attitudes that belittle women and trivialize violence against women.

If you have abused your intimate partner but have not been ordered into a domestic abuse program, or if you fear you have violent tendencies, volunteer to attend a program in your community. Go for the information, and get the help you need before your behavior escalates. I know many men who have built solid friendships through these programs. Like the supportive relationships often formed between recovering alcoholics, friendships developed in a domestic abuse program can help men who are committed to changing. Together men can grapple with personal issues and support each other in their commitment to remaining nonviolent.

In many communities men are getting together, albeit in small numbers, to talk about masculinity, domestic abuse, and how to prevent gender violence. Get involved for yourself. You can make a contribution toward reducing and ending men's violence against women.

New Definitions of Masculinity

Our understanding of masculinity is defined by our culture. At an early age we are exposed to expectations of what boys are supposed to be and what emotions they are allowed to express. Failure to live up to these expectations can be met with ridicule and scorn that leave an indelible mark on us as adult males. Think back to your childhood experiences. You may have been a bully who tormented boys who didn't "measure up" or "fit in." Conversely you may have been victimized by one or more boys (or perhaps girls) in grade school, middle school, or high school. Many men remember standing by when they were boys, afraid to intervene, as others were humiliated and abused. And this behavior doesn't always stop after high school. An astonishing 79 percent of male college athletes are subjected to hazing in the form of beatings, being tied up, being forced to wear embarrassing clothes, being made to drink to excess, or sexual assault. Similar behavior is commonplace in the military. Some claim that this conditioning is necessary to shape young men and women into a state of preparedness for war or to toughen them for competitive sports.

The rites of passage for boys maturing into men are steeped in cultural norms. Historically initiation rituals in many societies involve pain tolerance, endurance, or dangerous activities.

Whether imposed institutionally or via peer pressure, many boys and young men take extreme risks by driving cars or motorcycles recklessly, drinking excessively, getting into fights to defend their honor, or engaging in life-threatening stunts, often while intoxicated.

In the book *Violent No More* I interviewed Hector, a former Army Ranger who battered his wife. He explained his warrior mentality:

> So killing and fighting were what I was about. When I wasn't in combat, I'd be picking fights in bars in the towns near our installations. If someone messed with me, I'd pop him in the face and take him down. I'd fight other GIs in bars in Savannah or wherever we were stationed. We would actually go looking for fights. I'd tell my buddies, "That guy looks like he's tough. He's the cowboy I'm taking down today."

After Hector was arrested and subsequently completed a domestic abuse group, attended college, and obtained a degree in counseling, his attitudes about masculinity changed:

> When I work with men who batter, I know how difficult it is to get through the denial, blaming, and minimizing. I engage the men I work with and challenge their perceptions that they are the victims. I go back to a strength that I believe we all have. In our culture there are different ways of viewing masculinity—positive and negative. One value that I think is important is courage. That's not limited to men, but it is valued in male culture. And I don't mean like courage to fight or to do something reckless. I talk about how much courage it takes to become vulnerable. How much courage it takes to turn back into your shame. The courage it takes to take responsibility for your behavior.

In many ways men are in a state of crisis. If fearlessness, strength, and "power over others" are the only characteristics of manhood, that leaves no room for men to be compassionate, gentle, and nurturing. Because of narrow, destructive stereotypes such as these, men in growing numbers are seeking a healthier definition of masculinity, one that allows them to feel their emotions and to have healthier relationships with their intimate partners, their children, and their male friends.

As I've pointed out, when girls and women are hurt or rejected, generally speaking they handle their emotions very differently than men do. You don't often see a woman picking up a gun and killing her family members and then turning the weapon on herself. Nor do you often see a woman committing carnage at her place of employment because of a slight or because she lost her job. We don't see many girls taking out their aggression on fellow students and teachers by committing premeditated murder at schools. Although female violence and gang activity are increasing, the number of murders committed by girls and young women pales in comparison to the number committed by boys and young men, sometimes for minor indiscretions.

We men can define masculinity for ourselves. Our new definitions can include many important qualities that are sadly missing from conventional expressions of masculinity. *Let's examine some traditional masculine characteristics. How did they influence you? Are they getting in the way of your having a more satisfying life?*

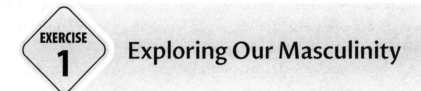

EXERCISE 1

Exploring Our Masculinity

Before beginning make sure you're in a quiet place where you won't be interrupted. Take some deep breaths to relax and clear your mind.

Part 1: Please review the following example exercise.

1. Think of your childhood. Remember your role models from movies and TV shows; remember the games you played; remember what you learned from your father (good and bad), from sports, on the playground, at school. How would you describe your boyhood role models and the definitions of masculinity you learned as a boy? What were some of those qualities?

   - *provider for the family/patriarch*
   - *good father/wise/helpful*
   - *courageous/bold/brave/gutsy*
   - *physically strong/tough*
   - *smart/clever*
   - *"scoring" with women*
   - *being able to defend yourself in a fight*
   - *not being too vulnerable/never crying*
   - *never losing to a girl/woman*
   - *risk taker/audacious/effective*
   - *aggressive/forceful/hard hitting*
   - *not feminine/not a wimp/not weak*
   - *being okay with your masculinity*
   - *chivalrous/brave/not cowardly*
   - *being successful at all costs*
   - *being willing to defend your "honor"*
   - *virile/macho*

2. How would you describe your definition of masculinity today? What has changed?

- *I'm not as controlling as I used to be.*
- *I don't have to settle things through violence.*
- *I'm working on being more vulnerable.*
- *I'm not as envious about other people's success.*
- *I'm working on being more intimate and open with my new partner.*
- *I'm trying to be a better dad.*
- *I'm more aware of how sexist beliefs are damaging.*
- *I don't feel that I have to prove myself to be a man.*

Part 2: Please answer the following questions.

1. Think of your childhood. Remember your role models from movies and TV shows; remember the games you played; remember what you learned from your father (good and bad), from sports, on the playground, at school. How would you describe your boyhood role models and the definitions of masculinity you learned as a boy? What were some of those qualities?

_____

_____

_____

_____

_____

_____

2. How would you describe your definition of masculinity today? What has changed?

_____

_____

_____

_____

_____

_____

_____

> If you're in a domestic abuse group, discuss this exercise together, preferably in small groups. Each participant should talk about what he learned from the exercise.

A Closing Thought

Our childhood experiences have had a powerful influence on us. We can't pretend that the intense pressure most men experienced as children and teenagers to "man up" didn't have a negative impact on us as we matured. The effects of these cultural expectations need not define you. You can decide what qualities of masculinity work for you in your quest to become a more positive and complete man.

Allowing yourself to be sensitive and nurturing does not diminish your masculinity. Allowing yourself to feel makes you more human and compassionate. You become a better father, a closer partner, and a stronger friend. In fact, in many ways allowing yourself to feel helps you gain greater courage, strength, and fortitude.

Challenging Entitlement

What do we mean when we use the term "male entitlement"? It's essentially the idea that men expect certain privileges based on their gender. In an interview I conducted for a documentary I wrote called *With Impunity: Men and Gender Violence,* the late Ellen Pence, a leader in the field to end gender violence, said:

> I think it's important not to individualize what is in fact a social phenomenon. Individual men beat women. Individual men rape women. Individual men participate in trafficking. Their proclivity to abuse an intimate partner or sexually assault a woman comes not from them as an individual, but rather it comes from their growing up as males in this society with this notion that they are entitled to what they want, when they want it.

In the same film, Michael Kimmel, author of *Guyland* and other books on gender and men's violence against women, said:

> I always think it's important to have a historical perspective. It's not just our personal history or our family history. It's not a question of whether our family at some time in history owned slaves or whether I have ever personally raped or beaten a woman. It's really the cultural legacy that I carry with me without even knowing it. It's sort of like an invisible knapsack of privilege—you walk through the world and you don't even know you're wearing it.

Male entitlement is both blatant and subtle. The more obvious forms include an expectation that it's men who should be the CEOs of businesses and heads of organizations. That men deserve to make more money than women and should be promoted because they are smarter, stronger, more logical, and better leaders. Other obvious forms of male entitlement include the rigid gender roles we explored earlier in this workbook, in which men believe they deserve (by the very nature of their gender) to be the head of the household. And as we discussed in the exercise on sexual respect, some men believe they are entitled to sex if they buy their date dinner, if she's flirtatious, or if they simply want it.

More subtle forms of male entitlement include the physical space some men occupy—for example, spreading their legs or sprawling out while on a bus or subway, in a meeting, or at home. Some men dominate a discussion or interrupt a conversation without thinking. Many men are convinced of the correctness of their position and defend it aggressively. Men are usually seen driving the family car with their female partners on the passenger side even though their partners are fully capable of driving.

Many men in our domestic groups get defensive when they hear the term "male entitlement" or "male privilege" applied to their experiences. They may claim that women have as much power as, if not more power than, men. Their partners may earn more money than they do. Some men claim that women use sex as a way to manipulate men. It's okay to struggle with what may seem like contradictions.

This exercise is not meant to condemn men or masculinity but rather to help you be aware of how male entitlement is damaging to both women and men. Some of the examples may not apply to you; they illustrate the variety of issues being worked through by men who are changing. *Let's explore entitlement from a broad cultural and personal perspective.*

> Before beginning make sure you're in a quiet place where you won't be interrupted. Take some deep breaths to relax and clear your mind.

Part 1: Please review the following examples of statements, assumptions, and beliefs that reflect male entitlement (rights or expectations of men's roles) in our society.

a) In the home/family

- *Women are better at housework.*
- *Men don't change diapers unless necessary.*
- *Men don't clean bathrooms.*
- *If a man doesn't provide the majority of child care, his masculinity isn't challenged.*
- *If a man does provide the majority of child care, he's praised.*

b) In the workplace

- *Men are more trusted as the CEO/CFO in a company.*
- *Men are better suited for jobs in law enforcement, fire fighting, construction, the military, etc.*
- *There isn't pay inequity.*
- *Promotions are based on performance, not gender.*

c) In dating and social activities

- *Women who dress "suggestively" are asking for it.*
- *A man isn't condemned for sleeping around. Women who do are called "sluts."*
- *If a woman is intoxicated, she's "fair game."*
- *If a woman is raped by someone she knows, she will usually be blamed.*
- *Men typically drive the car.*

d) In the community

- *Women who are sexually harassed are seductive or in the wrong place.*
- *Men don't have to worry about walking alone.*
- *Women should carry whistles and pepper spray and take self-defense classes.*

e) In society/culture

- *Men ask women to smile, use terms like "kiddo."*
- *The use of gendered language (e.g., "businessman," "freshman," "God the father," etc.) is normal and acceptable.*
- *Watching pornography is harmless. (Many people share this view, even though mainstream pornography increasingly portrays men being sexually violent and degrading toward women.)*

Part 2: Please answer the following questions.

1. Make a list or think of statements or assumptions that have reflected *your* beliefs about male entitlement (rights or expectations of men's roles) in society.

   a) In the home/family

   _____

   _____

   _____

   _____

   _____

   b) In the workplace

   _____

   _____

   _____

   _____

   _____

   c) In dating and social activities

   _____

   _____

   _____

   _____

   _____

d) In the community

_____

_____

_____

_____

_____

e) In society/culture

_____

_____

_____

_____

_____

2. In light of the statements, assumptions, and beliefs you listed in #1, what are you willing to change in your life?

_____

_____

_____

_____

_____

> If you're in a domestic abuse group, discuss this exercise together, preferably in small groups. Each participant should talk about what he learned from the exercise.

A Closing Thought

Sexist attitudes and a belief in male entitlement should be rejected. As a father how would you react if your daughter were being sexually harassed? What emotions would you have if she were taken advantage of sexually while at a college party? What would you think if she were beaten by her boyfriend? Sexism contributes to a man's decision to use violence in an intimate relationship and to exploit women.

On some level all men benefit from male violence, whether we wish to or not. Even though I try not to be sexist, my experiences are shaped by a sexist culture. Men have a responsibility to be agents of change, and the world will be a better place because of our efforts.

Getting Involved: Making Commitments to Social Change

Community institutions have largely been silent on the topic of gender violence. We don't often hear ministers, rabbis, or imams condemning domestic violence or challenging men in their congregations to reject sexism and entitlement. We don't often hear teachers, coaches, and administrators at high schools or colleges address sexual violence unless an incident occurs at their school. We don't see politicians speaking out against gender violence unless a horrific event happens in their community. What would happen if leaders in our community institutions were to address men's violence against women head on? What would happen if they were to make ending gender violence a priority?

Whether or not you are in a leadership position, as a man you have a voice in your community. Ask the counselors in your domestic abuse group how you can get involved in efforts to address gender violence. You might be surprised to learn that men and women are recognizing gender violence as a serious social problem and are discussing solutions. Students on college campuses, violence-prevention groups, battered women's shelters, domestic abuse programs, and faith-based organizations are confronting these issues. Of course, getting involved may take you out of your comfort zone a bit, but perhaps you can find solidarity with other men who are breaking their silence—who realize that ending gender violence requires men to get involved.

Some people claim that an end to gender violence will never happen. For instance, many individuals point to prostitution and assert that it's the "oldest profession" in the world and that men will always want to "purchase" women for sex. On the other hand, what would happen if the demand to buy sex declined or disappeared entirely? What would happen if men didn't feel they were entitled to "purchase" women for their sexual pleasures?

Other social problems have been successfully confronted by concerned citizens. Although the world is still dangerous, the need to control the proliferation of nuclear weapons is now recognized by almost all nations. Pollution of the environment was once considered a part of economic progress, but today this notion is challenged by environmentalists, the health community, and the public, who expect clean water to drink and clean air to breathe. As women and men continue to confront cultural and gender norms in an organized manner, we will continue to see change.

The key is for men to get involved. Prevention of gender violence is what I call the "next frontier." Men—especially men who have stopped abusing women, such as you—are in a perfect position to engage other men and boys about why on so many levels domestic and sexual violence are wrong. You have experienced the consequences of your violence—not just getting in trouble but maybe the loss of your relationship and the estrangement of your children.

I interviewed Chuck Derry from the Men's Action Network on the topic of prevention for my documentary *With Impunity: Men and Gender Violence.* He explained:

Primary prevention is figuring out how we stop the violence before it starts, which means changing the cultural norms. The thing that hasn't happened with primary prevention is to change the organizational practices that support sexual and domestic violence. When we think about primary prevention, we're really looking at a fifteen-year-old boy who wakes up in the morning and starts walking through his world. What are the messages he gets? When the radio alarm goes off, what music is he listening to? What are the lyrics? When he opens his eyes and looks around his bedroom, what are the posters on his wall, and how many of those sexually objectify women? When he pulls his pants on and goes to the bathroom, what's the marketing? What messages from advertisements tell him that to be a man you are entitled and expected to be sexually aggressive or dominant with women?

Primary prevention means reshaping the cultural environment into one in which boys and men can develop safe, healthy, and equitable relationships with girls and women.

Why is there so much male silence about men's violence? When we start to address men's violence against women, we start to examine the underpinnings of sexism, organizational power, and interpersonal power. It's easier to believe it's just an individual problem of some men abusing and harming women, but that attitude lets nonabusive men off the hook.

As men, we aren't forced to look at how we use power. We can choose to ignore gender-based injustices and disparities. Yet our silence supports those disparities and sustains men's unearned privileges. It is those privileges that I believe keep men from challenging the status quo.

As men we should take the initiative and work with other men and women to confront sexism and violence—not as a way to get approval from women, but because it is the right thing to do. Now that you've come this far, why not commit to going a bit farther by getting engaged with your community?

When I was first exposed to the ideas presented in the book *Violent No More* and in this workbook, it was a transformative experience for me. It still is. Recognizing how sexism permeates our culture and influences both men and women is powerful stuff. Hopefully during the course of your domestic abuse groups and while completing the exercises in this workbook, you've had some "aha" moments. An aha moment is a defining incident, thought, or realization that allows you to gain insight or wisdom into a problem. Like many of the men in our domestic abuse groups, I continue to struggle with my own sexism and sense of entitlement. But now that I have this increased awareness, it's hard not to be alert and sensitive to the impact of the gender violence that is all around me. Awareness means that you and I have choices about whether to act or speak up, even if doing so is uncomfortable. Once you've had an aha moment, it's difficult to go back. It's hard to remain a bystander.

Bystander intervention is a prevention strategy that involves both taking direct and indirect actions and also engaging our sons and other men about the harm of gender violence. On a college campus or at a bar, it might mean reporting an incident of sexual harassment or intervening directly or indirectly (informing people in authority) if you believe a sexual assault is imminent. In social or business situations, you may let someone know that a joke about rape or "wife beating" is inappropriate and explain why. Fathers and mothers can expand their "birds and bees" talk with their sons and daughters to include a discussion about why it's wrong for men to sexually take advantage of girls and women. If you know that a friend or family member is abusing his intimate partner, you can find the appropriate time to have a discussion with him, if he is willing.

Of course, this isn't always easy. Confronting someone in certain situations can be dangerous to yourself and others. Remember that it's not necessary for you to be a hero. In social situations in which a woman is being mistreated, there are usually men and women besides you who are also uncomfortable. On some college campuses, seminars are held to help men and women brainstorm about effective bystander interventions. Challenging a man who is making sexist comments or jokes and thinks he's being amusing may elicit his defensiveness, but if you are respectful, and if you consider in advance (by yourself or with others) the best way to handle such situations, your intervention can be a learning experience for him. Similarly, trying to engage a friend or family member about his domestic abuse might bring a response from him that you're meddling in his private business. True enough. But you've been there, and so he may be open to hearing what you have to say.

Still, despite your increased awareness, you have to decide in each circumstance whether intervening is going to be effective and safe. Bystander intervention isn't an exact science. There are plenty of times when I have remained silent because after assessing the situation, it didn't appear that my intervention would be helpful. Sometimes in retrospect I wish I had intervened or said something. As men we need to sort through the reasons for our silence.

Let's examine some of the reasons for our silence and consider how we can stop being bystanders.

EXERCISE
3

Why Are We Silent?

This following exercise can be done in your domestic abuse group. If you're not in a group you can still complete the exercise.

> Before beginning make sure you're in a quiet place where you won't be interrupted. Take some deep breaths to relax and clear your mind.

Part 1: Please review the following example exercise.

Participants break into groups of five or six, preferably seated at round tables. One person volunteers to take notes. Each person at the table describes an incident in which they heard a sexist comment or witnessed harassment or overtly abusive behavior toward a woman or women and didn't intervene.

1. Describe the incident. What was the nature of the harassment, incident, or sexist comment? How many people were there? Men or women?

    I was at a party, and everyone was pretty intoxicated. One woman was really drunk, and some of the men were clearly trying to get her to drink more. It was clear that some of the men intended to take advantage of her the drunker she got.

2. What were you doing?

    Mostly watching and drinking.

3. What did you think about what was occurring?

    I could tell what was going on. It was uncomfortable, but it was a party, and everyone was having a good time.

4. What options did you think you had?

    I'm not sure. I suppose I could have said something, but I chose to ignore it.

5. What stopped you from intervening or motivated you to intervene?

    Maybe fear. These guys were intimidating in some ways, and no one else seemed to care, not even the other women.

Part 2: Please complete the following exercise.

Participants break into groups of five or six, preferably seated at round tables. One person volunteers to take notes. Each person at the table describes an incident in which they heard a sexist comment or witnessed harassment or overtly abusive behavior toward a woman or women and didn't intervene.

1. Describe the incident. What was the nature of the harassment, incident, or sexist comment? How many people were there? Men or women?

_____

_____

_____

2. What were you doing?

_____

_____

_____

3. What did you think about what was occurring?

_____

_____

_____

4. What options did you think you had?

_____

_____

_____

5. What stopped you from intervening or motivated you to intervene?

_____

_____

_____

After about twenty minutes, ask the small groups to conclude their discussion. The note-taker reports back to the larger group on the general themes of the discussion without talking about the specific examples.

Next, as a large group discuss how men who find themselves in similar situations can respond differently. List several examples, and discuss the steps that men might take and what the implications of their interventions might be.

_____

_____

_____

_____

_____

A Closing Note

Increasingly, people as individuals and as part of community institutions are recognizing the need to change the bystander mentality. As stated, some college campuses are training students and faculty in how to prevent sexual assault at parties by, for example, intervening when young men are taking advantage of inebriated young women. Some businesses and organizations are training staff to recognize the signs of domestic abuse—for example, when someone appears afraid, is being stalked, or has visible marks or bruises. Staff should also be trained to recognize when someone is exhibiting possessively jealous behavior at the workplace by making threats on the phone, sending threatening texts and e-mails, etc. Some businesses are training staff to recognize signs of child prostitution (trafficking). There are many ways in which community institutions and individuals can contribute to the prevention of gender violence.

Social Change Activities

We can address violence against women in our community in many ways. Men can take a more active and visible role in confronting sexual and domestic assaults. We can join neighborhood crime watches, participate in anti-rape marches, and organize community meetings. We can initiate dialogue in our schools, churches, local governments, unions, professional associations, and community clubs. We can write letters to newspapers; talk to our friends; publicly confront judges who refuse to take domestic abuse cases seriously; and lobby our mayors, city council-ors, state legislators, and members of Congress for tougher laws to protect women who have been abused.

In many communities men have created organizations to take action against gender vio-lence. You can find out more about what's available in your community from your domestic abuse group, through local colleges and universities, or by going online. Also see the Resources section at the end of the workbook.

> Before beginning make sure you're in a quiet place where you won't be interrupted.
> Take some deep breaths to relax and clear your mind.

Part 1: Please review the following example exercise.

1. What will you commit to doing to create social change on gender-violence issues in your community?

   I will get active in my college fraternity and organize a meeting on gender violence.

   I will have conversations with my fellow students about sexism, appropriate behavior at parties, being responsible, etc.

2. What obstacles might you encounter, and what are some ways you could overcome those obstacles?

   Potential obstacle: I might be rejected or ridiculed by other male students.

   How to overcome the obstacle: Strategize ahead of time about how to respond to possible verbal ridicule. Line up allies for support before the meeting.

Part 2: Please answer the following questions.

1. What will you commit to doing to create social change on gender-violence issues in your community?

_____

_____

_____

_____

_____

2. What obstacles might you encounter, and what are some ways you could overcome those obstacles?

Potential obstacles:

_____

_____

_____

_____

How to overcome the obstacles:

_____

_____

_____

_____

A Closing Thought

When I witness how men often behave at bars, parties, sporting events, and social gatherings, and when I see how men are portrayed in television commercials, I'm stunned that more men aren't embarrassed. We have an image of men as living in a perpetual state of adolescence. In some cases the depiction is justified. Still, men should be appalled. Through our behavior—or our silence—we perpetuate a belief that sexism and the exploitation of women are harmless. They aren't. Many men reject the way our culture exploits women and enjoy respectful and equal relationships with women. But too often we men are silent when we encounter sexist messages about how men relate to women. It doesn't have to be that way.

Creating Change in Your Community

Perhaps you're feeling inspired to organize an event in your community to recruit other men and women to the work of gender-violence prevention. The following group exercise can help you get started.

1. Community institutions can be enlisted in efforts to challenge societal and cultural norms that contribute to men's violence against women. Create a PowerPoint slide listing the following institutions or write them on poster board. Brainstorm within the group about what, specifically, each of them can do to promote prevention efforts.

   - faith organizations (churches, temples, synagogues, mosques)
   - athletic groups
   - neighborhood groups
   - colleges and universities
   - middle schools and high schools
   - the business community
   - the criminal justice system
   - fraternal organizations
   - violence-prevention organizations
   - the media
   - the medical community
   - family

2. Break into small groups. Ideally each small group will have a representative from at least one of the institutions listed above, or the group's participants will have an interest in engaging one or more of the institutions. Brainstorm to develop plans for meeting with leaders of the various institutions. For example, in the faith community, plan to talk with a minister, priest, rabbi, imam, or other spiritual leader.
   Use the following questions as guidelines for your discussion:
   - Do the institution's leaders see gender-based violence as a problem?
   - Can they think of prevention strategies in which they might want to get involved?
   - Is there a way they can engage their congregations in discussing this issue?
   - Would they be open to sponsoring an event?

3. Work to develop a concrete plan. What steps will be taken, and who will take them? Who will be responsible for keeping the group on task? How will you measure success?

A Closing Note

The documentary I wrote, *With Impunity: Men and Gender Violence,* explores gender-based violence by looking at the historical roots of men's violence against women, the pillars that allow oppression to occur, the influence of our culture on men and boys, the backlash against the gains women have made, and the paths toward continued change. I have shown the film nationally and internationally. Men and women of all ages, races, and ethnicities have attended the screenings. After viewing the film we always have stimulating discussions about what community institutions need to do to address gender violence. People are genuinely concerned and want to get involved in some capacity, but there hasn't been an organized effort. Fortunately there is a growing awareness that we all have a role in addressing domestic abuse, sexual violence, and trafficking. Slowly people are stepping up and breaking the silence. The human and economic costs of doing nothing are unacceptable.

In Conclusion

To the Men Who Have Completed This Workbook

The exercises in this workbook are designed to help men in domestic abuse groups gain insights into the types of positive and affirming behaviors that are part of intimate relationships. They also challenge men to think more critically about their past abusive behavior with an eye toward recognizing other choices they could have made in their relationships.

Over the years I've heard countless haunting stories told to me by men who have caused incredible pain to their intimate partners. Some admitted their violence and abuse, and others continued to minimize their actions or blame their intimate partners.

I remember some men in my groups telling me that they wished they'd known what they learned in our groups before they got involved in an intimate relationship. They didn't have a relationship instruction book. The messages they internalized from their childhoods and from the culture had a powerful influence over the things they believed in as men: entitlement in relationships and using violence to settle disagreements. At the time they didn't see any other choices.

If you've completed the exercises in this workbook, you should have a clearer understanding of how you got to this place. Some men feel ashamed at what they have done. This is natural. Some men can't believe they made the choices they did. This is understandable and is part of the learning process and a key element in changing. Some men still harbor anger and resentment toward their partners or ex-partners. This is unfortunate. Despite your perceptions of what your partner did, you made the choice to use violence and other abusive behaviors. If you can't get past that first step (taking responsibility), you will have a difficult time changing. You will have a tough time reconciling with your current partner. If you begin a new relationship, you are more likely to repeat the behaviors of the past.

You know now that domestic abuse is more than just physical violence and that you must stop the pattern of intimidation, coercion, making threats, and controlling your intimate partner's life. You know that you have the tools to be respectful, supportive, and loving. You know that you can resolve disagreements with your partner by negotiating in a fair manner and compromising. You can have an equal relationship if you're willing to do the hard work required. You have to ask and answer the following questions:

- What do I have to give up?
- Will I take full responsibility for my behavior?

- What do I have to do to change?
- What personal risks am I willing to take?
- How will I stay true to my commitment to remaining nonviolent?
- Will I seek help when I need it?
- Will I use the tools I've learned in my groups and in this workbook?
- Am I willing to be accountable for my past behavior?
- Will I commit to an equal relationship with my current (or future) partner?

I have seen men make profound changes in their lives. Whether the motivation came from what they learned in their domestic abuse groups, the loss of their relationship, or the alienation of their children, these men have taken the often difficult steps of unraveling the sexist beliefs and attitudes that contributed to their use of violence. They have made the very personal decision that they don't always need to win or be in control. They now resolve conflicts without being violent, abusive, or controlling because they fully understand the self-defeating consequences of their past behaviors. They have become empathetic and realize they have the capacity to be in a loving relationship.

You have taken the first step in your long journey, but you can't stop now. Stay focused on the commitments you've made to remaining nonviolent and nonabusive. Ask for help if you need it. Use the exercises in the workbook to keep focused on your goals. Stay involved, and use what you've learned to reach out with a helping hand to other men. I have seen men make incredible transformations as intimate partners, fathers, and friends because they had the courage to change.

To the Counselors Who Have Used This Workbook

Often a fine line separates those of us who provide counseling in domestic abuse groups from the men who are participating. We've all been socialized in a culture that values power and accepts as an everyday reality the sexist thinking that we challenge in our groups. All of us have engaged in at least some of the abusive behaviors that men who batter use to control their partners. To challenge the status quo requires that we challenge ourselves.

In many ways, applying theories and using approaches that ignore the *intent* of violence and focusing instead on violence as a result of stress, anger, childhood trauma, or an inability to express feelings would be easier than what is required to change the long-held beliefs that many men have about male entitlement, women, and the use of violence to control another person. It would be easier to solely teach anger-management skills, and the men would prefer it. It would be easier to run therapy groups in which men could talk about their feelings, personal problems, and acts of violence without our reporting them to the court. The men would prefer this, too. Many counselors believe that reporting a group member to the court for using violence while he's in the program shuts down the rest of the group. This is true. But to fail to hold group members accountable for continued acts of violence is a form of collusion and negates a key principle of our work: the safety of victims.

As counselors and facilitators who run domestic abuse groups, we are in a unique position. We can challenge men to explore their beliefs about masculinity, entitlement, and violence to settle conflicts. We can engage men in dialogue without being confrontational or shaming. Men in our groups stand a greater chance of changing if we believe that each man has the capacity to change—but *they* must take that first step.

To the Women Who Have Participated in These Exercises (or Are Considering Doing So)

Although the book *Violent No More* and this workbook are written to men, many women whose partners are in domestic abuse groups want to know what their partners are learning. In fact, getting such information is critical if you're going to stay with your partner. Some women have found the insights in the book *Violent No More* and the exercises in this workbook to be the exact formula they had been hoping for. They can now assess whether their partners are serious about making changes—or simply going through the motions to satisfy them or the court.

For your own safety and decision-making about whether to stay in your relationship, you should be monitoring, assessing, and evaluating your partner's change process. You may want to work with a victim advocate or communicate with the counselor in your partner's domestic abuse program before participating in any of the exercises presented in this workbook. Ultimately you need to decide:

- Has your partner committed to and followed through on not using violence?
- Do you feel safer?
- Has he stopped using threatening, intimidating, and coercive behavior?
- Do you feel greater autonomy since he completed his groups and the exercises in this workbook?
- Is he being respectful and supportive?
- Is he working on being a good parent?
- Is he willing to negotiate and compromise with you?
- Has he stopped blaming, minimizing, and denying what he did in the past?
- Is he changing his beliefs and attitudes about women and relationships?
- Does he accept your anger and listen to your concerns?

If you decide to stay with your partner, I hope the exercises, stories, and ideas in the book *Violent No More* and in this workbook have been helpful. As you know, you are not alone. I often tell men who *want* to change that they are on a journey. Women who have been abused by an intimate partner are also on a journey—a journey of healing and empowerment.

If you have shared your story with an advocate, a counselor, or friends and family, you know that you weren't responsible for the violence. Most women never expected to be assaulted the first time. They usually never expected the next acts of violence either. I've heard women tell me that if their husbands or boyfriends ever hit them they'd be right out the door. You know that it's never quite that simple. Regardless of your economic status, level of education, strength, or reputation, it's easy to get trapped. It's likely (if you're reading this workbook) that you've called the police or obtained a civil protection order against your partner. You may have separated from him because of the violence or discussed your situation with an advocate. You've taken the first step: You got help. You now know that you have more options than you once thought.

If you stay with your partner, you deserve an intimate relationship that is free of violence and is grounded in love, respect, and equality.

Finally, reader, no matter what brought you to this workbook, I challenge you to become more involved in your community in addressing the issue of violence against women. Our community institutions are surprisingly silent about this complex social problem. The men and women who have been touched by domestic abuse, as well as the practitioners who work in this field, can and should challenge the bystander attitude that says gender violence only happens to certain people in certain neighborhoods. Nothing could be further from the truth. Let us commit to prevention. Whether we focus on modeling egalitarian relationships to our children, teaching respect and equality in our schools, challenging male entitlement on college campuses, or confronting sexism in the workplace, we can each make our community, and by extension our world, a more peaceful place.

Resources

The following resources may be useful for men, women, advocates, counselors, and other interveners reading this workbook. Most states in the United States and provinces in Canada have organizations that provide referral information for victims of domestic and sexual violence and contact information about domestic abuse counseling agencies in their jurisdictions. Included in this list are national organizations that provide training, technical assistance, and resources in specific areas of domestic abuse prevention and intervention.

Resources for Men

National Domestic Violence Hotline
(800) 799-7233   TTY: (800) 787-3224
www.thehotline.org

Counseling Programs for Men Who Batter
Batterer Intervention Service Center of Michigan
www.biscmi.org

United Kingdom, Help Line
www.nationaldomesticviolencehelpline.org.uk

Men's Advice Line, United Kingdom
www.mensadviceline.org.uk

Resources for Women

National Domestic Violence Hotline
(800) 799-SAFE (7233)   TTY: (800) 787-3224
www.thehotline.org

National Coalition Against Domestic Violence
A list of state coalitions can be found through their website.
www.ncadv.org

Child Abuse

The Childhelp National Child Abuse Hotline
(800) 422-4453
www.childhelp.org/pages/hotline-home

Counseling/Mental Health Help and Assistance

Crisis Services/24-Hour Help Hotline—Crisis Call Center

(800) 273-8255

www.crisiscallcenter.org/crisisservices.html

National Suicide Prevention Lifeline

(800) 273-8255

www.suicidepreventionlifeline.org

Technical Assistance

U.S. Department of Justice, Office on Violence Against Women (OVW)

www.justice.gov/ovw

Resources for Advocates

Praxis International, Inc.

A nonprofit research and training organization that works toward the elimination of violence in the lives of women and children.

www.praxisinternational.org

Danger Assessment

The Danger Assessment instrument created by Jacquelyn Campbell can be used by domestic violence advocates and health-care providers.

www.dangerassessment.org

Veterans and Military Personnel and Their Families

The following are useful resources for military personnel, veterans, victim advocates, and practitioners in the domestic abuse field.

- Eligible veterans can receive free screening and treatment for PTSD and other combat-related mental health issues, traumatic brain injury (TBI), and substance abuse at VA facilities. However, services related to intimate partner violence were not being provided in every VA facility at the time this book was written.

- Active-duty military personnel can receive free mental health services through Department of Defense and TRICARE health-care resources.

- *Returning from the War Zone: A Guide for Military Personnel,* published by the VA National Center for PTSD, contains information on what to expect when returning from combat and how to help military members better transition back to home life. The guide also provides a list of resources. The guide can be found at: www.ptsd.va.gov/public/reintegration/returning_from_the_war_zone_guides.asp.

- *Returning from the War Zone: A Guide for Families of Military Members* is a similar guide for family members. It can be found at: www.ptsd.va.gov/public/reintegration/returning_from_the_war_zone_guides.asp.

- Active duty military and veteran families can contact **Military OneSource at (800) 342-9647,** twenty-four hours a day, seven days a week. Some states have their own hotline programs. Individuals who are attached to a military installation can contact the installation's victim advocate, the Family Advocacy Program (FAP), law enforcement, and/or IPV/domestic violence programs in the local civilian community. Contact information for installation FAPs can be found online using the Installation Locator on the Military OneSource Homepage: www.militaryonesource.mil.

- Additional information for understanding the military response to IPV/domestic violence can be found in the handbook *Understanding the Military Response to Domestic Violence: Tools for Civilian Advocates* at: www.bwjp.org/articles/article-list.aspx?id=30.

- Advocates (military and civilian) will find the e-learning course *Safety at Home, Intimate Partner Violence, Military Personnel and Veterans* useful in providing services to military-related families experiencing intimate partner violence (a link to the program can be found at www.bwjp.org/elearning_course .aspx). Funded by the Avon Foundation, the five-module program was produced by the Battered Women's Justice Project (www.bwjp.org).

You may also contact a local program in your community that provides services for men who batter.

For domestic abuse programs, staff should have referral information if they believe that a court-mandated offender may have post-traumatic stress disorder or traumatic brain injury (TBI). Many of the current screening tools don't provide the kinds of questions that a domestic abuse program uses to assess battering and risk to an intimate partner. It may be that the court-mandated offender ordered into your program has co-occurring conditions and therefore should be screened for each.

The following websites offer information on PTSD and screening:

The Department of Veterans Affairs National Center for PTSD
www.ptsd.va.gov/professional/assessment/screens/pc-ptsd.asp
www.ptsd.va.gov/professional/provider-type/doctors/screening-and-referral.asp

National Center for PTSD (Lists other PTSD screens)
www.ptsd.va.gov/professional/assessment/screens/index.asp

Standards for Batterer Intervention Programs/Domestic Abuse Programs

Batterer Intervention Service Center
Provides full listings of U.S. programs.
www.biscmi.org

RESPECT United Kingdom
http://respect.uk.net/work/work-perpetrators-domestic-violence/accreditation

Other U.S. Organizations

Asian and Pacific Islander Institute on Domestic Violence
www.apiidv.org

Battered Women's Justice Project
www.bwjp.org

Domestic Abuse Intervention Programs
www.theduluthmodel.org

Education for Critical Thinking
http://educationforcriticalthinking.org

Faith Trust Institute
www.faithtrustinstitute.org

Family Violence Prevention Fund
http://nnedv.org/resources/nationalorgs/9-fvpf.html

Futures Without Violence
www.futureswithoutviolence.org

Gender Violence Institute
www.genderviolenceinstitute.org

Institute on Domestic Violence in the African American Community
www.idvaac.org

Institute on Violence, Abuse and Trauma
www.ivatcenters.org

Jewish Women International
www.jewishwomen.org

LGBTQ Relationships and Abuse: National Domestic Violence Hotline
www.thehotline.org/2012/06/lgbtq-relationships-and-abuse

LAMBDA GLBT Community Services
www.lambda.org

Manavi
A women's rights organization committed to ending all forms of violence and exploitation against South Asian women living in the United States.
www.manavi.org

Mending the Sacred Hoop
http://mshoop.org

Minnesota Center Against Violence and Abuse
www.mincava.umn.edu

National Association of Drug Court Professionals
www.nadcp.org

National Center for Elder Abuse
www.ncea.aoa.gov

National Center on Domestic and Sexual Violence
www.ncdsv.org

National Center on Protection Orders and Full Faith & Credit
www.fullfaithandcredit.org

National Clearinghouse for the Defense of Battered Women
www.ncdbw.org

National Latino Alliance for the Elimination of Domestic Violence (ALIANZA)
www.dvalianza.org

National Network to End Domestic Violence
www.nnedv.org

Rape, Abuse & Incest National Network (RAINN)
https://rainn.org

Resource Center on Domestic Violence: Child Protection & Custody
www.ncjfcj.org/content/view/129/250

National Council of Juvenile and Family Court Judges
www.ncjfcj.org

Prevention/Social Change

Here are some initiatives that have demonstrated positive results, as well as a list of national and international organizations that are working on primary prevention strategies:

BEST Party Model
The BEST Party Model is a step-by-step guide for college students on how to throw parties that are safe, respectful, and fun for women. It provides an opportunity to change the social environments that contribute to sexual and domestic violence at colleges and universities. The model has also been a tool for students, staff, and faculty to shape campus spaces such as residence halls, locker rooms, student lounges, and classrooms, with the goal of creating an overall campus environment that equally empowers male and female students, faculty, and staff.
www.menaspeacemakers.org

A Call to Men
A Call to Men is a national organization providing training and education for men, boys, and communities. It partners with schools, universities, corporations, governmental units, and social service agencies to end all forms of violence and discrimination against women and girls. It also promotes healthy and respectful models of manhood and has consulted with the National Football League, the United States military, and the media on ways institutions can prevent gender-based violence.
www.acalltomen.org

Education for Critical Thinking (ECT)
Education for Critical Thinking explores meaningful ways to challenge community institutions to do more to end gender-based violence, including domestic violence, rape, trafficking, and violent pornography. It produced the documentary *With Impunity: Men and Gender Violence* and provides training nationally and internationally.
www.educationforcriticalthinking.org

Futures Without Violence
Futures Without Violence provides technical assistance to organizations around the country that are engaging men to prevent violence against women and girls. It has also organized the Coaches Leadership Program, which equips coaches to talk with athletes about respect for women and girls and remind them that violence doesn't equal strength.
www.futureswithoutviolence.org

Men Can Stop Rape
Men Can Stop Rape is an international organization that mobilizes men to use their strength to create cultures free of violence, especially men's violence against women. It has developed education programs, public-awareness messaging, and training. Its approach is grounded in the social-ecological model for primary prevention.
www.mencanstoprape.org

The MENding Project

The MENding Project asks traditionally male-run or male-oriented businesses to provide free or reduced-cost goods and services for victims/survivors of sexual and domestic violence and trafficking. The MENding Project provides educational materials for business owners to help them answer questions about their participation in the program, including window and countertop display cards that promote the message of men's collective responsibility to end sexual and domestic violence in the community.
www.themendingproject.org

MenEngage Global Alliance

MenEngage is an alliance of nongovernmental organizations that seek to engage men and boys in effective ways to reduce gender inequalities and promote the health and well-being of women, men, and children. This international project has developed a "tool kit" for good practices to carry out advocacy campaigns and act as a collective voice to promote a global movement of men and boys engaged in and working for gender equality.
www.engagement.net

Men Stopping Violence

Men Stopping Violence is a national training institute that provides communities, organizations, and individuals with the knowledge required to mobilize men to prevent violence against women and girls. It offers an innovative community-restoration program for men who have completed their domestic abuse program and are interested in giving back to the community.
www.menstoppingviolence.org

MensWork

MensWork is a grassroots organization that develops and supports male leadership to prevent bullying, sexual harassment, rape, dating violence, domestic violence, and sexual exploitation by engaging men and boys through an array of programs and community events.
www.mensworkinc.com

Mentors in Violence Prevention

Mentors in Violence Prevention provides education and training on the prevention of gender violence, bullying, and school violence. Its training is focused on the "bystander model," which empowers students to take an active role in promoting a positive school climate.
www.mvpstrategies.net

PreventConnect

PreventConnect is a national project of the California Coalition Against Sexual Assault. Building on the strengths of the rape crisis and domestic violence movements, its goal is to advance primary prevention of sexual assault and relationship violence, using various forms of online media to connect people and ideas to stop the violence before it starts.
www.preventconnect.org

Prevention Through Athletics

The Minnesota Men's Action Network has collaborated with high-school sports leagues to design an online course for coaches to help them embed gender equity and sexual and domestic violence prevention into team culture.
www.menaspeacemakers.org/programs/mnman

Promundo

Promundo is a Brazil-based organization that promotes caring, nonviolent, and equitable masculinities and gender relations in Brazil and internationally by conducting research, developing transformative inter-

ventions and policies, and carrying out advocacy to achieve gender equality and social justice. It engages teachers, health-sector workers, businesses, and community organizations.
www.promundo.org

Sonke Gender Justice Network
The Sonke Gender Justice Network is a South African–based NGO (nongovernmental organization) that works across Africa to strengthen government and civil society organizations and to support men and boys in taking action to promote gender equality, prevent domestic and sexual violence, and reduce the spread of AIDS.
www.genderjustice.org

White Ribbon Campaign
The White Ribbon Campaign is a global organization that examines the root causes of gender violence, creating a cultural shift that challenges negative, outdated concepts of manhood that lead to violence against women. It positively engages men, young men, and boys through education, outreach, technical assistance, and partnerships.
www.whiteribbon.ca

XY
XY is a website focused on men, masculinities, and gender politics. It's a space for the exploration of topics related to gender and sexuality, and the daily issues of men's and women's lives, and for practical discussions of personal and social change.
www.xyonline.net

These are just a few of the national and international organizations that are doing important prevention work. Their websites can give you ideas on how you can make a difference in your own community. You don't have to be a big nonprofit or NGO to make things happen locally. Programs in your own community, state/province, or schools may already be doing this work. Talk with like-minded men and women, and start organizing!

International Programs

Advocates for Human Rights
http://theadvocatesforhumanrights.org

Amnesty International USA, Women's Human Rights Program
www.amnestyusa.org/our-work/issues/women-s-rights

Women's Aid (United Kingdom)
www.womensaid.org.uk

Books

The following books can be a good resource for you to learn more about gender violence and change:

Adams, David. *Why Do They Kill? Men Who Murder Their Intimate Partners*. Nashville, TN: Vanderbilt University Press, 2007.

Aldarondo, Etiony, and Fernando Mederos. *Programs for Men Who Batter: Intervention and Prevention*. Kingston, NJ: Civic Research Institute, 2002.

Bancroft, Lundy. *When Dad Hurts Mom: Helping Your Children Heal the Wounds of Witnessing Abuse*. New York: Berkley Publishing Group, 2004.

Browne, Angela. *When Battered Women Kill*. New York: The Free Press, 1984.

Campbell, Jacquelyn C. *Assessing Dangerousness: Violence by Batterers and Child Abusers*. New York: Springer Publishing Co., 2007.

Davies, Jill. *Safety Planning With Battered Women: Complex Lives/Difficult Choices*. Thousand Oaks; CA: Sage Publications, 1997.

Dobash, R. Emerson, and Russell P. Dobash. *Violence Against Wives*. New York: The Free Press, 1983.

Edleson, Jeffery L., and Richard M. Tolman. *Intervention for Men Who Batter*. Thousand Oaks, CA: Sage Publications, 1992.

Faludi, Susan. *Backlash: The Undeclared War Against American Women*. New York: Crown Publishers, 1991.

Ferrato, Donna. *Living With the Enemy*. New York: Aperture Books, 1991.

Freire, Paulo. *Pedagogy of the Oppressed*. New York: Continuum, 1992.

Funk, Russ. *Stopping Rape: A Challenge for Men*. Gabriola Island, BC, Canada: New Society Publishers, 1993.

Garbarino, James. *Lost Boys: Why Our Sons Turn Violent and How We Can Save Them*. New York: The Free Press, 1999.

Gilligan, James. *Violence: Our Deadly Epidemic and Its Causes*. New York: Grosset/Putnam, 1996.

Gondolf, Edward. *The Future of Batterers Programs: Reassessing Evidence-Based Practices*. Lebanon, NH: Northeastern University Press, 2012.

Gondolf, Edward. *Men Who Batter: An Integrated Approach for Stopping Wife Abuse*. Learning Publications, 1985.

hooks, bell. *Ain't I a Woman: Black Women and Feminism*. Cambridge, MA: South End Press, 1981.

Jones, Ann. *War Is Not Over When It's Over*. New York: Metropolitan Books, 2010.

Katz, Jackson. *The Macho Paradox*. Naperville, IL: Sourcebooks, Inc., 2006.

Kimmel, Michael. *Guyland: The Perilous World Where Boys Become Men*. New York: HarperCollins, 2008.

Kimmel, Michael. *Manhood in America: A Cultural History*. New York: Oxford University Press, 1998, 2006, 2012.

Kivel, Paul. *Men's Work: How to Stop the Violence That Tears Our Lives Apart*. New York: Hazelden/Ballantine, 1992.

Kristof, Nicholas, and Sheryl WuDunn. *Half the Sky*. New York: Vintage Books, 2009.

Lissette, Andrea, and Richard Kraus. *Free Yourself from an Abusive Relationship: Seven Steps to Taking Back Your Life*. Alameda, CA: Hunter House, 2000.

Martin, Del. *Battered Wives*. Volcano, CA: Volcano Press, 1981.

Paymar, Michael, and Ellen Pence. *Education Groups for Men Who Batter: The Duluth Model*. New York: Springer Publishing Company, 1993.

Pence, Ellen, and Melanie Shepard. *Coordinated Community Response to Domestic Violence: Lessons From Duluth and Beyond*. Thousand Oaks, CA: Sage Publications, 1999.

Pleck, Elizabeth. *Domestic Tyranny*. Champaign, IL: University of Illinois Press, 2004.

Richie, Beth. *Compelled to Crime: The Gender Entrapment of Battered Black Women*. New York: Routledge, 1996.

Schechter, Susan. *Women and Male Violence: The Visions and Struggles of the Battered Women's Movement*. Boston: South End Press, 1982.

Schechter, Susan, and Ann Jones. *When Love Goes Wrong: What to Do When You Can't Do Anything Right—Strategies for Women with Controlling Partners*. New York: HarperCollins, 1992.

Stark, Evan. *Coercive Control: The Entrapment of Women in Personal Life*. New York: Oxford University Press, 2007.

Websdale, Neil. *Understanding Domestic Homicides*. Lebanon, NH: Northeastern University Press, 1999.

9 781630 267612